THE SECRET PSYCHOLOGY OF FREEMASONRY

For My Brother

TRAVIS

It was an honor to speak at your lodge.

i

First Edition in Paperback Published in 2011

Published by Starr Publishing, LLC
Colorado Springs, CO 80917

ISBN-13: 978-0615497709
ISBN-10: 0615497705

The Secret Psychology Of Freemasonry

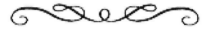

Alchemy, Gnosis, and the
Science of the Craft

by

Cliff Porter

Edited by R. Gregory Starr

Starr Publishing, LLC
Denver ★Colorado Springs

Dedication

I would like to dedicate this work to those men and women who have sat upon the Porter Porch and helped me find the answers I was looking for. The long conversations, the shared smiles, the laughter, and the insights I have gained in those special moments perched upon my simple rattan chairs have been rare treasures. The Scotch and cigars have been good, the memories have been priceless.

- Cliff Porter

Table of Contents

Acknowledgments

A Mason can only be a fulfilled and active Mason when his family supports that journey. For this reason I want to thank my wife, Eva, and my son, Stephen, who are always beside me.

To Greg Starr, my friend, Brother and editor. Thank you so much Brother for the hard work and helping hand. I enjoy our friendship, fellowship and working together.

To Paul Dickerson, Tim Hogan and Brazen Serpent Press for making the leather bound edition of this book a work of art and for selecting this book for such a wonderful endeavor.

To Enlightenment Lodge No. 198, the singularly best lodge in the world. You are the greatest and best of men. You are Masonry.

To the Southern Colorado Consistory for being a place of education, growth and encouragement.

To Dr. Stephen Rhoads and the International Training Academy of Linguistics and Kinesics for your ground breaking work in the field of subconscious communications; I cannot thank you enough; you have given me freely of your knowledge and I have learned much from you.

To those who kept the Secret alive and the flame alight. I hope this does you some level of honor as we all try to find our way on this journey to the heart.

Special thank you to Melanie Herd who corrected errors of the first edition for me

Foreword

by Jim Tresner

The last 48 years have been an interesting time in Freemasonry. When I joined the Lodge, Masons were typically middle-aged and older men. Most Lodges occasionally had a dinner (Masonic green beans remain notorious to this day—open a large can of the least expensive green beans you can find; place seasonings on a table nearby, but not in the beans; walk past the pot, quietly muttering the word "bacon," and boil vigorously for 6 to 8 hours). Most Lodges quietly did some charitable work. No one ever talked to their friends about the Fraternity. It was more than a civic club with a ritual—but sometimes not much more.

Then women's lib ambushed us. Most of us were not at all sure what to make of it, but we tried. After all, perhaps that was responsible for lower membership numbers. And so, at the urging of Grand Lodges, the local Lodges added more family activities, encouraged the ladies to visit, etc. At Guthrie Scottish Rite, we spent many hours and many dollars planing activities for ladies at the Reunions. We brought in special entertainment for them, created and staffed a child care center, so they could bring their children with them. We knew we had to do all that, because when we surveyed the members, they told us that was important. And the ladies "stayed away in droves."

When we talked to the members (as opposed to surveying them) we found out that they never told their wives of the activities, because they simply did not want them there. This was supposed to be guy time. And that was fine with the wives, most of whom figured that they had a rare weekend to themselves.

The next big change happened in the late 1990's when the fundamentalists (not to be confused with evangelicals) once again decided that Freemasonry was the great Satan. It was serious. Many Brethren were forced by their churches to choose between Freemasonry and their denomination. We did the best we could at the time, but, in retrospect, much of what we did at least smacked of appeasement. We tried to convince them that we were just a harmless group of old men, doing a little charity work and finding ways to occupy our time. Some Masonic organizations even changed what we called our buildings, getting rid of the words "temple," "cathedral," and "mosque," and turning into "centers," at least officially.

Without meaning to, without even noticing it, we spent half a century throwing away almost everything it really means to be a Mason.

But of late, there has been a sea-change. Mostly led by younger men, some Masons have been standing up and saying, "We're taking it back." They are proclaiming that Freemasonry is, and is intended to be, an initiatic organization. Through such things as Masonic Restoration, the Traditional Observance Lodges, and in Masonic fora across the nation, Masons are taking back their heritage, proclaiming once again that the purpose of Freemasonry is the development and transformation of the individual Mason, and that while Masonry is not a religion concerned with the salvation of the soul, it is a spiritual quest, concerned with each man's discovery of his relationship to the universe.

Cliff Porter, good friend and author, is at the forefront of this movement. There is a saying among musicians that when Beethoven wrote the *Missa Solemnis*, he took God by the beard and said, "You WILL be glorified if I say you will." So, in a sense, it is with Brother Porter. He is not afraid to charge the barricades, banner in one hand and sword in the other. He does it fraternally and with compassion, but he does it. It makes his both an important and a refreshing voice in the Masonic world. I had the pleasure of reading this book in draft and I was honored to be asked to write a foreword for the publication. It is filled with thought and insight.   It is also filled with the passion of a Mason who is determined that hiding one's head in the sand is an undignified posture for an ostrich, and an unforgivable one for a man.

- Jim Tresner

Preface

I thought it might be valuable to launch straight into the premise of this book, so the reader understands where the journey is supposed to go from here.

I offer the following:

Within Freemasonry, there is contained a secret teaching which amounts to a dynamic system of psychology present in all the most potent of the mystical traditions since time immemorial. Further, this complex system of psychology identifies both the personality typology and primary senses of perception as they relate to communications in human interaction. Additionally, the numerological correspondences interlaced through Craft ritual contain information designed to provide the keys to perfecting communication.

When a person can master their own typology, understand the systems of perception, and combine this with key communication techniques, he can unlock the mysteries of mankind. We can detect deception, influence others, and speak a special language to each individual, so that they see, hear, and experience our language, as if uniquely crafted to be spoken only to them.

We may scoff at such an idea, given our current approach to Masonry in America. However, it is also part of this premise that the deeper meanings of our ritual have been lost to us in a myriad of minutes, mediocre food, and unrelated charity work. Charity work for its own sake has little to do with the true charity of heart, as practiced by those who have come to a realistic view of themselves and others. When the true connections of human beings, one to another, become apparent, charity becomes as beautiful and as selfish as it is intended to be. This may seem a strange statement, but Masonry, much like charity, is a selfish journey shared with others.

During the height of the Mysteries in the Middle East, Africa, and Europe, one who had mastered this special understanding of this most ancient Craft was revered like a God and made High Priest or messiah, depending on the culture at hand. In other cultures he became the Tau or the Lao Tzu. So it was, that in the temple at Delphi we read, "Know thyself and though shall know the universe and the Gods."

Before we delve into a study of how this philosophy developed, how it made its way into Masonry, what it is, and how to use it, I will make the case that Masonry is special and intended to be such. I propose that the Masonry we recognize today is a sad reflection of the true wonders that Masonry is intended to impart.

Chapter I

The Situation Today

Let us begin with one of the most common phases in Masonry today, "Masonry makes good men better." The origin of the phrase is unknown to me and when it made its first appearance is uncertain. However, by 1923, it was clearly engrained as an idea in the American Masonic culture, as H.L. Haywood would write,

> "'Good and true men.' How simple yet how profound are these time-worn adjectives! They are not qualities that

glitter but they are, in their completeness, as rare as many that do! If it be asked why Masonry does not accept bad men in order to make them good, it replies that such is not its function, for it has a unique purpose of its own to carry out, and its demands are made with that in view. One organization cannot attempt everything. The reformation of men is left to other agencies."[1]

This demonstrates not only was the idea of improvement upon *good* firmly entrenched, but arguments concerning Masonry's role in the reformation of the bad had, likewise, already been well established.

What a bold statement to make; that we take something that is already good and improve it.   The proper implementation of such an idea seems in a direct conflict with the numerous papers written regarding the degradation of Masonry through initiation of the undeserving, immoral, or otherwise unfit persons.

In 1858 Albert Pike, the much misunderstood, under-read Masonic magus, would address the membership of the Grand Lodge of Louisiana saying,

"It would need no argument to show that to the Masonic Order itself, as to any other order or association, however unpretending and unimportant, intestine dissensions, struggles for the possession of power, jealousies and heart-burnings must necessarily be harmful, retard its growth and progress, repel those who, if it were at peace within itself, would seek to approach its doors; and at first diminish and ultimately destroy its capacity for usefulness. If this were all that I desired to establish, I might say so much and at once conclude."[2]

Again we find the idea of only the good, maybe even the best of men, being the stone from which Masonry is to carve its perfect ashlars.

One might argue that the idea of "making good men better" is as old as the Craft itself. In the Comedies of Plautus from 1769 C.E. we find the words,

"...five few of those sort of plays our poets find, T' improve our morals, and make good men better. Now if the piece has pleas'd you, with our acting if you're content, and we have not incur'd Displeasure by it, give us then this token..."[3]

Not Masonic per se, but one could certainly make the argument given the choice of words.

Taking into account our current Masonic culture, is it hubris to believe that we can take a man considered decent, moral and good by his community and improve upon him? Perhaps, but we should ask ourselves how it was, that Masonry should come to the conclusion, that it is considered a given we do not reform the bad; rather, we improve the good, and we have the tools to accomplish it. So much so, Brother Pike provides allowing in the unworthy and unprepared can destroy the mechanism.

Although Masonry differs from jurisdiction to jurisdiction within the United States, the problems plaguing the current membership are common enough to inspire numerous blogs, papers, articles, and e-Masonic forums focused upon similar arguments, rants, and denunciations of the same issues as noted previously: minutes, bills, and boredom. Leadership conferences and various symposia are rife with concerns over membership, while passionate young Masons declare that membership is not the problem.

This places a necessary question before us, "If Masonry is to make good men better, if it is to improve, enlighten, or elevate the good man, what in a Masonic lodge meeting does this?"

For many North American Masons, the answer is, "not much if anything" in a Masonic meeting enriches the Mason or provides him with opportunities for introspection, self-awareness, and in so achieving said awareness, self-improvement.

This problem or condition of failing to find Masonry in Masonic lodges is not a new one. As early as 1835 in *An Exposition of the Mysteries or Religious Dogmas and Customs of Egyptians, Pythagoreans and Druids: With a inquiry into the origin and history of Freemasonry*, John Fellows writes:

> "The original object of the secret rites of freemasonry has been a subject of inquiry for upwards of six hundred years, and the enigma seems not to

have been satisfactorily solved. The initiated, as well as those without the pale of the order, are equally ignorant of their derivation and import. What mote it be? [sic] is a question as difficult of solution now as when first propounded by king Henry VI of England."[4]

Brother Manly P. Hall declares similarly in the *Lost Keys of Freemasonry*:

"The average Mason, as well as the modern student of Masonic ideals, little realizes the cosmic obligation he takes upon himself when he begins his search for the sacred truths of Nature as they are concealed in the ancient and modern rituals. He must not lightly regard his vows, and if he would not bring upon himself years and ages of suffering he must cease to consider Freemasonry solely as a social order only a few centuries old. He must realize that the ancient mystic teachings as perpetuated in the modern rites are sacred, and that powers unseen and unrecognized mold the destiny of those who consciously and of their own free will take upon themselves the obligations of the Fraternity."[5]

While it may be argued these are observations of the past, what Mason, arriving at the Craft today, finds what he should in the way of instruction within the doors of a lodge? We read of great mysteries and deeper meanings, yet philosophical education, in-depth study, discussion of the degrees, and ardent research into the true mystical characteristic of our allegories is given little, if any, consideration during an average lodge meeting.

Even from our educated Brethren, there comes little aid. It seems even the most studied in Masonry are contented to study the works of others from a purely historical standpoint. There are those for whom a well annotated and footnoted work of another is held to be the highest of Masonic pursuits. To declare a Masonic origin false and some allegory pretentious is the order of the day and, in their eyes, serves as proof of their love of Masonry. This does little except to falsely demystify the Craft for the sake of academic approval; but in the end, no matter what of the history of Masonry is uncovered or partially exposed, no answer for *how* Masonry is to improve and spiritually elevate an already good man is offered. There is little consequence in knowing the specific date of the first use of a particular sign or symbol, if the sign or symbol is never comprehended at a philosophical level, nor applied in the manner and form which causes the transformation of the man who has discovered the mechanism by which to inculcate it in his life.

We also have the closet prophet, who loves Masonry, loves philosophy, studies deeply and is contended to embitter himself against the establishment. He convinces himself that he is better served in deep contemplation than in trying to work within the systems of the Craft itself to ensure a fulfilling experience for all. He forgets that the system he rejects is what allows the philosophy he loves to be propagated throughout the globe. It is the system that gave birth to him as a Mason.

"It becomes my duty to inform you that you are not yet in possession of all the Secrets of a Master Mason, nor do I know that you ever will be."

There are claims that the esoteric cannot be shared in writing because it is "ineffable." While there may be some truth in this statement, as the experience is difficult or maybe even impossible to describe, the Sacred Truths of the Mysteries are very much available. To declare them "ineffable" is nothing more than a pretentious metaphysical way of avoiding the fact that you may not have the answer. It is easier to say that the answer is a secret or cannot be communicated, rather than admit that we have not found the answer for ourselves and fear that we may never find it.

It is not that historical study is in vain, but whether the current collection of degrees was born of stone masons or Templars does little to uncover the secret method by which its practitioners were improved. Those who claim an ancient origin for Masonry, such as Egypt or Atlantis, offer nothing even is such a hypothesis had been proven. It would still be a mystery why such a philosophy endured for so long, when its current incarnation devotes itself to reading minutes, paying the bills, or raising money for corporate charities. Why would Templar origins matter as we flip pancakes for pennies, then argue about how to spend them?

My brethren, there is a secret and extraordinary meaning in the degrees of Masonry. They contain a secret system by which a man may come to know himself deeply and honestly. They contain a secret system by which we may apply this understanding of ourselves to understanding others. They contain a secret system that identifies the tools of *perfect* communication upon which the Perfect Ashlar is built. They contain the tools that grant the power of persuasion and detecting deception. Once a Brother knows the truth about himself, he can discover the falsehood in others. To know the truth of a situation is power indeed.

Chapter II

The Mystical Traditions

So we can understand how Masonry came to its position as a keeper of an ancient mystical tradition incorporating a secret psychology of self, it is necessary that we discuss, at least briefly, the Mystical Traditions. This will not be an encyclopedic introduction to the Mysteries in hopes of filling space and creating an opportunity for footnotes, nor a valiant effort to convince you that Masonry is more ancient than it is. Whether or not Masonry is ancient matters little. What does matter is that Freemasonry is the current convention and vehicle of an eternal teaching, born in the consciousness of humankind to improve and better oneself. The evolution of a species drives only toward adaptation and improvement. The goal is not singular at any point. Evolution never drives toward perfection, it drives toward necessity, based on the current need. In much the same way, Masonry, and the mysteries that preceded it, drives toward accuracy, relevance and usefulness. This is why Masonry is a *progressive* science.

American Masonry seems so terrified of progression, that the only people who hate the idea of a new lodge forming more than anti-Masons are the Masons themselves. Nonetheless, we must acknowledge that Masonry is a progressive science and a relevant philosophy. When it ceases being so, it will die because it has failed to evolve. This is the way of things. For the time being, however, Freemasonry is just beginning to realize its real-time relevance in a world of traditionalized intolerance and new religious crusades.

The "Ancient Mysteries" is a broad term and can be taken in many ways. What we might call "mystical traditions" have existed throughout the world since man first formed societies and lived together in groups. It would seem that after forming groups, the first thing man did was to form sub-groups, and then keep those groups private. Masonry recognizes this pivotal point in the evolution of human consciousness with the very core of its teachings. This basic understanding concerning the creation of the societal unit is critical to understanding several foundational points to building our temple upon the secret psychology within.

Next, we will examine this teaching hidden within the Craft degrees, which was added at the end of Craft Masonry and at the beginning of publicly-known Speculative Masonry to serve as a guidepost to the teachings within the Fellowcraft degree. It is important to note the Fellowcraft degree was originally intended to be the highest of the degrees and contains the majority of the scientific psychological lessons.

In the Hebrew tradition, the first city ever built - the first real society - was erected by Cain after being cast from the Garden. We are all, in this way, indebted to Cain for our present material existence and the formation of societal groups. This also means, in our present material condition, we remain cast out from the Garden, separated from the Presence of the Divine, and living among the material in the societies formed by the first true descendant of the material, in that he descended into the material and gave way to the primal urges within himself.

What this means is that Cain (קַיִן) was the first to turn from the singular thing that separates humans from the beasts: consciousness. Cain gave himself over to the more primal urges. He hoarded, he hated, and he murdered. In giving himself over to this "lower" nature, he was cast away from the Divine Spark within himself and would build the dualistic world of the demiurge.

This story is most clear in the Book of Jubalees in Chapter 4:

> "And in the third week in the second jubilee she gave birth to Cain, and in the fourth she gave birth to Abel, and in

the fifth she gave birth to her daughter Awan. And in the first of the third jubilee, Cain slew Abel because they accepted the sacrifice of Abel, and did not accept the offering of Cain. And he slew him in the field and his blood cried from the ground to heaven, complaining because he had slain him. The Lord reproved Cain because of Abel, because he had slain him, and he made him a fugitive on the earth because of the blood of his Brother, and he cursed him upon the earth. And on this account it is written on the heavenly tables, 'Cursed is he who smites his neighbor treacherously, and let all who have seen and heard say, 'So be it; and the man who has seen and not declared the same, let him be accursed as the other.' And for this reason we announce when we come before the Lord our God all the sin which is committed in heaven and on earth, and in light and in darkness, and everywhere.....

And Cain took Awan his sister to be his wife and she bare him Enoch at the close of the fourth jubilee. And in the first year of the first week of the fifth jubilee, *houses were built on the earth, and Cain built a city*, and called its name after the name of his son Enoch.

...thereof, Adam died, and all his sons buried him in the land of his creation, *and he was the first to be buried in the earth.* And he lacked seventy years of one thousand years; for one thousand years are as one day in the testimony of the heavens and therefore was it written *concerning the tree of knowledge: 'On the day that ye eat thereof ye shall die.'* For this reason he did not complete the years of this day; for he died during it. At the close of this jubilee Cain was killed after him in the same year; for his *house fell upon him* and he died in the midst of his house, and he was *killed by its stones*; for with a stone he had killed Abel, and by a stone was he killed in righteous judgment."[6]

From this Hebraic allegory, some important points that have made their way into Masonry should be noted, as they support the premise that the mystical instruction within this allegory is the same philosophy found in many traditions, but for our purposes, in Masonry.

It is worth considering that after his fall into the primal existence of the material, Cain settles in the Land of Nod, which is to say in the land of wandering (לְנדוד). The original intent of this word can mean or imply, "to lose normal mental contact or stray in thought."[7] This is in keeping with the lesson of the allegory, that in the forming of the first society among men was to descend into the material and have a false perception and to deny consciousness.

Nod is said to be East of Eden. So, the starting point by which we might begin to understand our condition is *in the East.*

It is Adam, and not Abel, who is the first to be buried or returned to the earth. This is important, as Abel was clearly the first to die, yet he was not buried within the earth, or more importantly - from the standpoint of terminology - he did not "return" to the earth as his father would.

This points to Adam as an icon for mankind or Adam Kadmon, the first archetype. In the End, the Beginning is found. This is why the Masonic journey ends with an explanation of the beginning or foundation of societal knowledge, the solid foundation in which to build our spiritual house. This is the true or real value of the Master Mason degree.

Cain dies by a *stone* from his house falling down about him. It is the rough stone of his society that falls *just after* the death of Adam and a new spiritual temple can be built, as with the Tree of Knowledge. Thus, the answer remains both within ourselves and in our original state; the story of reintegration. Our true self recognizing that the rough ashlar was never our true condition.

Cain's son is Tubalcain, or the Metal Smith. As the son ushers in the New Age, so Tubalcain ushered in the Bronze Age from the Age of Cain, or "Stone" Age. So, a Mason learns that, as a Master Mason, he too must usher in a New Age to stand within an assemblage of Masons.

~ ~ ~

Masonry does not share its philosophies with the Hebrew Tradition alone. After the first societies were established, mankind built "houses" or groups and sub-groups. This gave way to the system that would give birth to the Mysteries.

The group caused mankind to question, "What are we and what are we doing here?" When not everyone wanted such questions asked, we formed the smaller group and asked, "What are we doing within this larger group we call the world?" These groups would further focus their devotees' attentions and we would begin to ask, "What am I, and not we, doing within the group?" This gave the individual the courage to ask, "What am I doing here, what am I, and how am I both disconnected from society, but a member of it all at the same time?"

Thus the Entered Apprentice is given the keys to ask those questions within himself. The Fellowcraft is given the tools to answer those questions and the Master Mason is given the way in which to teach, because we learn "from whence it came."

The teaching mechanism that we use in Masonry is the conferring of degrees. It is within the Mystical Traditions, or "the Mysteries" collectively, that we find the origin of the system for concealing the teaching of self-awareness within a system of degrees; a system designed to provided a tiered instruction, as the human mind prepares itself to receive a Truth which might be lost on the otherwise unprepared mind. Just as a house cannot be built with purely rough stone, lest it fall and kill its builder, as in the case of Cain; the human mind must build its understanding upon the proper foundation of understanding.

Samuel Angus (1881 to 1943) was an ordained Presbyterian clergyman who wrote what are still considered the quintessential books on the Mystical Traditions and their relationship to Christianity, and therefore, the Western Esoteric Tradition. The books are *The Environment of Early Christianity* (1914), *Mystery-Religions and Christianity* (1925), and *The Religious Quests of the Graeco-Roman World* (1929).

From Angus' meticulous accounts and historical research, a picture of the Mystical Traditions is formed.

We know that they were the following:

- Secretive. They were so much so, that even from their initiates, we have very little in writing. No direct expose of the degrees of any of the traditions in their entirety, and almost nothing from the priesthood or leadership of the traditions exist. Often, there are not even records from the Tradition's founder, such as in the case of the Pythagoreans, Socrates, or Jeshua: we do not have a single word written by any of them.

- Initiatic. There were elaborate initiations, but these are only referenced in tantalizingly small quantities from various initiates.

- Ritualistic. Great labyrinths, such as those in Minos; massive structures, such as pyramids; underground crypts and lodges, such as with the Mithraic mysteries found throughout the Roman Empire; and the massive mounds of the Celts - are all evidence of ritualistic ceremonies of great import.

- Focused on Self-Awareness. The central focus of the various approaches is centered on self awareness and a knowledge that surpasses the knowledge of the masses. We have the temple at Delphi and its declaration that in knowing oneself you have access to knowledge of the Gods and of the universe.

The priesthood of the pagan traditions were said to have insights that made them like the Gods and gave them communion with Deity. In some of the Gnostic schools, Moses is said to have had additional commandments that contained knowledge for which the world was not ready. Thus, the high priesthood kept this knowledge secret. The knowledge of the high priesthood in the Judaic traditions was considered so powerful, that prior to entering communion with Deity or the presence of God, the priest tied a cable tow around himself, leaving one end outside the temple. If the priest was found unworthy of seeing or experiencing the "manner and forms" of Divine Communion or "the temple," he would be killed and drug from the temple by the cable tow. In Masonry, the cable tow has the same mission, with the exception that the candidate is not said to die, but to remain in darkness.

So, what was this great knowledge that must be structured in degrees and could metaphorically harm those who were not prepared to receive it? What was it that could, perhaps, even cause physical harm in a world that was not ready to receive it?

Beginning with the rise of the Christian church to power, the systematic elimination of mystery religions, the more public pagan faiths, and even Gnostic approaches to Christianity, would eventually culminate in an accepted doctrine wherein self-awareness was considered so sinful, so harmful, and so heretical, it was punishable by death. Yet, whenever the pendulum of life swings to one extreme in its journey, there are always reactions to set it upon its return course. The Enlightenment Era of Europe was such an event: a growth of consciousness not seen in the world since 500 BCE.[8]

Contributing to an atmosphere beneficial to the ideas of the Enlightenment, the Protestant Reformation had wrested control of God from the Roman Catholic Church and removed the Church as the administrator of man on behalf of God. This allowed a flowering of humanistic thought, ushering in an *Era of Reason*, and a return to the time honored questions of, "Who am I and what am I doing here?"

This resurgence of Reason triggered interest and investigation of the same ancient mystical traditions that had been so long suppressed. Ancient Judaic verbal traditions, committed to writing by Greek-influenced Spanish Jews, were being distributed in Europe within certain circles and a new interest in Egyptian and Greek traditions had exploded, reviving the study of Neo-Platonism and Hermeticism.

This new melange of Science, Religion, Spirituality and Reason would bring about a new interest in Alchemy, the Science of Transformation. Alchemy, born in ancient Egypt ,was approached as a *speculative* art by ancient Greeks, such as Hippocrates.

It is with the birth of *Speculative* Alchemy that we will concern ourselves; but it would be foolish to believe that Alchemy is not also *Operative* and that the operations of Alchemy are not, likewise, important to an understanding of Freemasonry as a whole.

It would not be inaccurate to say that Masonry is Alchemy. Masonry is both operative and speculative, as it is with both labor and thought that a Mason can achieve mastery. For instance, the penalties cannot be understood from a Masonic perspective without researching Operative Alchemy. Brother Timothy Hogan details these operations in his work *The Alchemical Keys to Masonic Ritual.*[9] For instance, Brother Hogan is able to describe a spagyric operation in which an herb is harvested or torn out by its roots, placed in a sea of alcohol, then placed in a salt and sand bath, where it is agitated twice in 24 hours as part of the initial operation.

It is worth noting that Alchemy often refers to substances such as salt, sulfur, or mercury. However, the elements of Alchemy are Earth, Air, Fire, or Water, which often make up what we would describe as the "characteristics" of a substance.

Paracelsus wrote, "Man is a thinker. He is that what he thinks. When he thinks fire, he is fire. When he thinks war, he will create war. Everything depends if his entire imagination will be an entire sun, that is, that he will imagine himself completely that what he wants."[10]

So for the alchemist, Fire is the archetype of action, labor, and transformation.   Until something is broken down, seemingly destroyed, or prepared for initiation, it cannot be transformed.   It is where the idea of a "trial by fire" comes from.   This can be described as man's *intuitive sense.*

"The Alchemist"

Air is the archetype of spirit and refers not to the Soul as a Westerner might think, but to that which is connected to the Mind or the All.   This can be considered the thinking part of man.   It is in the elevation of the mind and consciousness where Air will later be used.   For, as in Water we are drenched in the subconscious, so in Air are we taken across the threshold to Reason and are no longer entangled in Superstition.

Water is the archetype of purification or dissolution which alludes to the fact that, through the corrosive power of gentle water, even the strongest metal yields. Water is, therefore, the alchemical element that will divest something of all its metallic substances, or false pretenses. Whereas Air is considered *thinking* in nature, Water is *feeling*.

Earth is the archetype of creation or the material. It is related to coagulation or the evaporation of one substance to form a new solid. It is critical in finding the new stone, one that is free from both superstition and the equally dangerous relativism. Many times, when seeking the Philosopher's stone, alchemists fail to coagulate, pretending the liquid is part of the whole so they do not have to apply the Fire, evaporating a myth they hold dear. Earth is associated with being in-tune or sensate, e.g., "I can't describe love, but I know it when I feel it."

From a Jungian standpoint, the alchemical elements, or archetypes, can be directly related to an ancient philosopher who would help give birth to speculative Freemasonry. Whether or not he ever intended to, Hippocrates took these same elements and broke them down to a microcosmic level, and then wrote his observations as part of his teachings. He was one of the first Western philosophers to do so and much of modern psychology and medicine are indebted to him. It would be inaccurate to claim Hippocrates as the originator of this line of thinking, however, as there are similar teachings in the Eastern philosophies of India which can claim a greater antiquity than the writings of Hippocrates. Many of these ideas were born in the river valleys of the Tigris and Euphrates and traveled to

India and gave birth to Hinduism;[11] others which remained behind gave birth to monotheism.

Hippocrates said that the human species was made up of four humors. These humors were identified as yellow bile, black bile, phlegm and blood.

Thus, by Hippocrates' own design, they are related to the hot, dry, wet and cold of the alchemical elements as follows:

YELLOW BILE = FIRE

BLACK BILE = EARTH

PLEGM = WATER

BLOOD = AIR

In its simplest form, Hippocrates' teaching said the composition of the humors within you determined your personality type. This idea of four distinct personality types remains true even today. Even more extraordinary is the fact that they are both the same personality types identified within the ancient mysteries and the same personality types clinical psychology recognizes to this day.

Hippocrates named the personality types Choleric, Melancholic, Phelgmatic, and Sanguine. They can be related to the previous examples as:

CHOLERIC = FIRE = YELLOW BILE

MELANCHOLIC = EARTH = BLACK BILE

PHLEGMATIC = WATER = PLEGM

SANGUINE = AIR = BLOOD

"Melencholia" by Albrecht Dürer

While these relationships may not seem remarkable by themselves, considering that the description given to each of the personality types has not changed from the time of Hippocrates and has remained an archetypal constant since the birth of human consciousness, it is noteworthy that each generation seems to remain ignorant of them, in large part, as has every preceding generation, and just as likely, so shall each subsequent generation.

The alchemist had recognized this remarkable truth of the nature of man, and indeed, the nature of the entire universe, and had tried to apply this knowledge in both spiritual and material operations.

As set up by the alchemist, these operations - both material and spiritual - numbered seven, tying it directly to the Second Section of the Fellowcraft lecture so common in the Preston-Webb rituals, and to the many references of a flight of winding stairs so common in many of the Middle Chamber lectures throughout the world.   Seven is the number of perfection, both operationally in Alchemy and psychology.   It takes six instances in number to develop a habit, and so it is at seven that we gain Mastery.

These operations and elements are also repeatedly referred to in the penalties of the three degrees.

In the Entered Apprentice penalty, we find Water and Earth; in the Fellowcraft penalty, we find Air; in the Master Mason, we find Fire.   In every aspect of Masonry, we find references to the alchemical operations of transmutation.

It is logical, therefore, if there is an allusion to transmutation, there must be an operation by which to achieve it.

Alchemical writings and practices allude to this as well, in that each operation requires the physical participation in the operation itself, or the material act - the labor of it - or the *operative* part, and the spiritual mindset of the practitioner, or *speculative* part.

The fascination with Alchemy, and the truths to be gained from it as a complete science, were no small pursuit in Enlightenment Era Europe.   It was the primary pursuit of the era's greatest thinkers.   The largest percentage of Isaac Newton's writings were dedicated to Alchemy.   Francis Bacon, Elias Ashmole, and several others were drivers of this time of Reason and the exponential growth of consciousness; all were involved in investigations of Alchemy.   Alchemy was widely respected and was termed the "Royal Art." It would eventually travel across the Atlantic to America, and there are   written communications from the alchemist Philalathes to Benjamin Franklin offering Brother Franklin the Philosopher's Stone.[12]

However, since there is not a vast amount of alchemical gold flooding the world markets, we must investigate what great mystery was found in Alchemy.   Why did it draw its teachings from ancient symbols and mystical traditions and why were these intriguing enough to become the central focus of the greatest men in Enlightenment Europe, and fascinate the founders of the United States? More importantly, how can believing people are made up of Fire, Earth, Water, and Air, whether associated with personality traits or not, be a valuable resource?

We can conclude that something valuable must have existed in the teachings and practice of Alchemy.   We know this because it would give birth to both modern psychology and the modern secret society, simultaneously displaying the "gold" it had found and concealing its true power.

We have also reviewed the ancient mysteries' teaching of the birth of society and the foundation of consciousness, and the allegories of both Masonry and the ancient Judaic traditions establishing the conditions necessary for the great creative questions to be asked, "Who am I, what am I, and what am I doing here?"

We will need to keep in mind the discussion surrounding Alchemy and our review of the mystical traditions as we continue.

Chapter III

Condemnation

As presented earlier, the ancient mysteries contained a set of practices similar in manner and form to modern Masonry. Also, we find that the ancient truth of the mysteries, the mystery itself, was likely tied to "knowing oneself" or self-awareness. As a natural reaction to the oppressive actions and growing abuses of the Church, the Reformation and Enlightenment exploded in Europe. In doing so, they ushered in a time of reason and investigation. The men responsible for this very special time in history focused much of their investigations on both the ancient mystical traditions and Alchemy, both operative and speculative.

These same men would be some of the first recorded Speculative Freemasons in the world and, I propose, this is how the philosophies of the ancient mysteries made it into the degrees of Masonry.

The degrees of Masonry are singularly designed to improve you. They have hidden knowledge; they turn lead to gold, both materially and spiritually.

The very reason this knowledge had remained hidden, flourishing only in the secret societies of enlightenment era Europe, was the penalty of death inflicted by the Church should one try to govern oneself physically, spiritually, or emotionally. To commune with the Divine without "paying for your ticket" through the Church was seen as the seeds of the Church's utter destruction.

This may seem an overstatement in regards to the Craft, but when the words of Pope Leo XIII are read, it becomes difficult to ignore the importance of secrecy to Freemasonry and the war upon self-awareness and self-governance still waged by the Church.

Humanum Genus

In the *Humanum Genus*[13] issued in 1884 by Pope Leo XIII, a clearer message could not be given. Pope Leo XIII was not the first pontiff to denounce Freemasonry or its principles. He was preceded by Popes Clement XII, Benedict XIV, Pius VII, Leo XII, Pius VIII, Gregory XVI, and Pius IX. In total, twenty papal bulls have been promulgated which, either in part or in their entirety, condemn Freemasonry. For the purposes of this narrative, I will cite sections from the *Humanum Genus*, following each with commentary relevant to the premise of this text.

In Paragraph 3 it states:

> "At so urgent a crisis, when so fierce and so pressing an onslaught is made upon the Christian name, it is Our office to point out the danger, to mark who are the adversaries, and to the best of Our power to make head against their plans and devices, that those may not perish whose salvation is committed to Us, and that the kingdom of Jesus Christ entrusted to Our charge may not stand and remain whole, but may be enlarged by an ever-increasing growth throughout the world."

In Paragraph 5:

> "The first warning of the danger was given by Clement XII in the year 1738, and his constitution was confirmed and renewed by Benedict XIV and Pius VII followed the same path; and Leo XII, by his apostolic constitution, Quo Graviora, put together the acts and decrees of former Pontiffs on this subject, and ratified and confirmed them forever. In the same sense spoke Pius VIII, Gregory XVI, and, many times over, Pius IX."

In the above paragraph, it is evident that the Church has been warring upon the philosophies of Masonry the instant those same philosophies became known to the Church.

In Paragraph 6:

> "For as soon as the constitution and the spirit of the Masonic sect were clearly discovered by manifest signs of its actions, by the investigation of its causes, by publication of its laws, and of its rites and commentaries, with the addition often of the personal testimony of those who were in the secret, this apostolic see denounced the sect of the Freemasons, and publicly declared its constitution, as contrary to law and right, to be pernicious no less to Christiandom than to the State; and it forbade any one to enter the society, under the penalties which the Church is wont to inflict upon exceptionally guilty persons...."

In Paragraph 8:

> "...We no sooner came to the helm of the Church than We clearly saw and felt it to be Our duty to use Our authority to the very utmost against so vast an evil. We have several times already, as occasion served, attacked [Masonry]... We described the ideal of political government conformed to the principles

> of Christian wisdom, which is marvelously in harmony, on the one hand, with the natural order of things, and, in the other, with the well-being of both sovereign princes and of nations. It is now Our intention, following the example of Our predecessors, directly to treat of the masonic society itself, of its whole teaching, of its aims, and of its manner of thinking and acting, in order to bring more and more into the light its power for evil, and to do what We can to arrest the contagion of this fatal plague."

In this paragraph, the Church does not equivocate in its condemnation of Masonry, as it has within its teachings the idea that a man cannot rule himself when it relates to his relationship with God or running his own government. One of the "sins" of Masonry that the Church so vigorously sought to stamp out was the idea of Democracy and self-rule, found in lodges long before it ever found its way into a modern system of government. Here is one piece of evidence that should give you pause the next time you seek to dismiss Masonry as nothing more than a men's club with a charitable slant and publicly declare that Masonry has no secrets. At worst, you are lying; at best you are ignorant of the truth.

From Paragraph 10:

> "Now, the masonic sect produces fruits that are pernicious and of the bitterest savour. For, from what We have above most clearly shown, that which is their

ultimate purpose forces itself into view - namely, the utter overthrow of that whole religious and political order of the world which the Christian teaching has produced, and the substitution of a new state of things in accordance with their ideas, of which the foundations and laws shall be drawn from mere naturalism."

The overthrow of the Church as a political mechanism is certainly in keeping with the ideas of freewill, but it has never been the concern of the Mason, and the Church knows this. What the Church also knows, and some Masons have forgotten, is the power of the freeman and free mind. The Church fears the principles inculcated in Masonry because these ideas lead good men to assemble and throw off the chains of oppression. Thus, it is not Masonry the Church should truly fear, but the free, educated man.

In Paragraph 11:

> "...*for the masonic federation is to be judged not so much by the things which it has done, or brought to completion, as by the sum of its pronounced opinions.*"

From this paragraph, it becomes apparent it is the *thoughts* and the *consciousness*, not the *actions*, of its members to which the Church objected. This is a critical point as it shows exactly why Masons assemble in private and once again offers evidence the Church recognizes something in the Fraternity, which its own members may well have forgotten: As the work of

Masonry lies in its speculative nature, so Masonry's secrets lie in the power of the mind.

In Paragraph 12

> "Now, the fundamental doctrine of the naturalists, which they sufficiently make known by their very name, is that human nature and human reason ought in all things to be mistress and guide...For they deny... [that] any teacher who ought to be believed by reason of his authority [alone]. And since it is the special and *exclusive duty of the Catholic Church fully to set forth in words truths divinely received, to teach, besides other divine helps to salvation, the authority of its office,* and to defend the same with perfect purity, it is against the Church that the rage and attack of the enemies are principally directed."

In this paragraph, the Church has claimed sole authority over the opinion of what is Truth and what must be believed based on its authority alone. Free thought is once again the sin of the Craft, and therefore, the teachings of self-awareness inculcated in the Craft are kept secret, even to some of its members, through the use of allegory and symbolism.

In Paragraph 13:

> "In those matters which regard religion let it be seen how the sect of the Freemasons acts, especially where it is

more free to act without restraint, and then let any one judge whether in fact it does not wish to carry out the policy of the naturalists. By a long and persevering labor, they endeavor to bring about this result - namely, that the teaching office and authority of the Church may become of no account in the civil State; and for this same reason they declare to the people and contend that Church and State ought to be altogether disunited. By this means they reject from the laws and from the commonwealth the wholesome influence of the Catholic religion; and they consequently imagine that States ought to be constituted without any regard for the laws and precepts of the Church."

Here the Masons are accused of supporting a democratic government and the separation of church and state.

In the preceding extracts, I hope the premise of this book has been sufficiently underscored: Masonry is special. It holds special truths and has had to keep these truths secret because they were considered deadly. Even after the ability of the Church to kill or destroy those opposing its views was removed, it did not cease its war upon those who set out to discover themselves and live as Free men - and Freemasons.

N.B. So that it cannot be said that I have edited the words of *Humanum Genus* for my own purposes, it has been made available unedited, in its entirety, and without my commentary as Appendix A at the end of this book. I encourage all to read it for themselves.

Chapter IV

Typology

In order for my claim that there is a secret psychology in Masonry to ring true, we must agree on what I mean by *psychology*. Therefore, when referring to psychology, I am specifically referring to *Jungian psychology*.

Carl Jung gleaned many of his ideas from both alchemy and the mystical traditions. Jung's studies were legitimized by the academic establishment and deemed separate from their mystical origins.[14]

The ideas which Jung removed from the metaphysical and made clinical, as well as their presence in Masonry, are important to the premise of this text.

The Archetype and Type

The Archetype can be considered the basic pattern or motif that makes up each individual within the greater construct of humankind. Jung provided that there were many archetypes, and it would be fair to think of them as our "psychic" genes. While the use, meaning and importance of each part of our DNA might be difficult to discern, their collective importance is commonly known to the layman. It would be fair to say that as DNA physically makes us who we are, so archetypes make us who we are *consciously* and *subconsciously*. So when we talk about archetypes, in many ways, we are talking about our mental building blocks.

In his writings, Jung would often refer to "common" or main archetypes. These were:

The Self - the regulating center of the psyche and facilitator of individuation; the representative of "that wholeness which the introspective philosophy of all times and climes has characterized with an inexhaustible variety of symbols, names and concepts."

The Shadow - the opposite of the ego image, that part of ourselves with which we have difficulty reconciling.

The Persona - the mask or the image we try to show the world.

The Anima - the feminine archetype within man's psyche.

The Animus - the masculine archetype within a woman's psyche.

These archetypes play an important role in all initiatic traditions. Jung said of initiation, "A man who has not passed through the inferno of his passions has never overcome them."[15] It is within systems of initiation that we first confront ourselves and then, through instruction, reconcile ourselves. We must first admit, embrace, and confront our passions in life, if we are ever going to subdue them. It can be said that we journey in circular motion upon the motif of our own Self, Ego, and Shadow, in the form of the Mosaic pavement. We glide upon the very nature of our archetypal self.

We then remove the symbol of the persona, the hoodwink, then, in good faith and after obligation, show our true self to our Brethren. We are guided by the Ego in the form of the Senior Deacon who carries the symbol of the Sun and Solstice, the alchemical wisdom, to assist in guiding us. The Deacon's role as the Ego is made even clearer in recognition that he never speaks when we are asked if we are making our decision of our own freewill.

The initiations are often kept to a singular gender, males in fraternity, females in sorority, so that the Animus and Anima, respectively, can make an appearance without judgement and the person can find balance in recognizing these hidden aspects.

Initiation - the passing of the threshold or the rite of passage - is the literal grasping of an archetype and shedding of the persona for personal growth. One of the greatest working tools found as part of this journey is the "type," which is not to be confused with archetypes.

A type could be defined as the personal expression of our archetype. As a consequence of the rite of initiation, the type becomes the outward manifestation of our individualized selves.

Personality types have many different names in our current culture, but this was not always the case.

Jung would revolutionize typology with his discussions of *introversion* versus *extroversion* and *rational* versus *emotional* types. The rational types are fact and detail oriented, the emotional can be said to be experientially or feeling oriented.

While typologies do not rule the informed initiate, they do drive our "natural" reactions to things. Our wants and needs, strengths and weakness, and reactions are driven by our typology. This is the circuitry that our reactions will follow if not intercepted by reason and focused attention learned through initiation.

Since Hippocrates, the names have changed, and since Jung, the public recognition of the power of typology in understanding one another has changed, but the types themselves have remained the same.

Jung brought the idea of extroversion and introversion to the forefront of psychology and divided the types by rational and emotional. Polar differences exist within all four personality types, but of the four, two are rational and two emotional. It might be said that the self aware man stands between these two poles as a key to awareness, which Jung called individuation, while the ancient mystics would have called it "ecstasy" and the ancient Christians would have called it Gnosis.

Several different systems have been developed to identify personality types. Some of these systems are extremely complicated and hundreds of questions long, charging hundreds of dollars per exam to administer; others have given cute and common names to the types so as to make them more memorable and more usable in daily life. For instance, the Christian author and lecturer Gary Smalley identifies the types as Lion, Otter, Beaver, and Golden Retriever. A common method used today by law enforcement in interview and interrogation is titled the DISC system and refers to the types as Dominant, Influencer, Steadfast, and Compliant or Conscientious.

For our purposes, I have chosen to name the types in the manner I use in teaching subconscious communications: the Why, When, What, and Who types. I utilize these because they answer the question most important to each of the types.

They might be understood this way:

YELLOW BILE = FIRE= CHOLERIC = DOMINANT = WHY

BLACK BILE = EARTH = MELANCHOLIC =STEADFAST = WHEN

PLEGM = WATER = PHLEGMATIC=COMPLIANT = WHAT

BLOOD = AIR = SANGUINE= INFLUENCER = WHO

First we will define the types and then we will discover how they are inculcated within the Craft and the power their understanding brings. This understanding is especially potent in Masonry, as it is paired with a secret teaching concerning the senses of perception.

After defining the types, we will discuss how to use the information we have learned and how to apply it in the ways of old; in ways that elevated men to the Priest Craft for their very knowledge of it. But before learning to run, we must first learn to walk.

We will examine each of the types individually before we discuss the practical application of the information we have learned, which we will do in a chapter dedicated specifically to that purpose. Much like the Entered Apprentice is instructed to listen, the Fellowcraft to learn and labor, and the Master to teach, we will follow a similar system with a belief that the instruction we receive in the Craft might have some actual value.

Choleric / Dominant / Why

Why's are fact oriented people; they are big picture people, but do not want to know about the feelings or experiences of the situation.

The "Why's" personality is forceful, direct and competitive. Why's make up 9 percent of the population. This is logical, as we know there can only be so many bosses, and our Why's are natural leaders.

When we discuss the strengths of the Why's, we could say that they are confident and willing to make decisions. They are very direct communicators and lend themselves to straightforward and succinct answers. Our Why's are a *Rational* personality type; because the "feelings" of others are not a priority for them, they give honest answers to questions. It does not cross their mind that when their wife asks, "Do I look fat in this?" she doesn't want an honest answer necessarily. What she might want is reassurance from her lover that she is still attractive to him. The Why is likely to give the answer, "Yes you look fat in the dress, but it's not the dress; it is primarily because you are overweight."

Why's work well on their own and tend to self-motivate. Because the Why is challenge oriented, they carry heavy work loads well and like to "accomplish" things. It is not that the Why loves their work, but they often work hard to "conquer" their assignments. Why's often stay busy and can get dangerous when they are bored. They have been referred to by Dr. Stephen Rhoads in his various lectures on Subconscious Communications[16] as having a "Fireman Mentality." Because the Why's learn early in life that fireman are heros, they also learn that you can only be a hero when there is a fire to put out. So, when a Why gets bored, they light fires so they can put them out and be a hero.

If you have ever had a boss who was a Why and things had started to settle down at work, to where it finally felt like you could catch a breather, the Why calls everyone together to talk about different "problems" they have discovered. Often they believe they are the agent who must "shake things up." Then, when work picks up again, their pet "boredom" projects often subside, and they will decide that their intervention has succeeded and the problem *they helped create* has been abated.

Why's are energetic and often the "go to" guys in any given situation. Why's like to work toward a goal, so they can define success and move on to the next challenge. For this reason, they will also seek out changes and variety.

Phrases that are common to the Why personality are:

- Why?
- If you want a job done right, you have to do it yourself.
- If you don't want an honest answer, don't ask the question.
- Sometimes you just have to be a *&^% to get the job done.

As all personalities have strengths, likewise, they have weaknesses. Here is where the personality types tend to compliment one another, in that, the strength of one personality type, is the weakness of another and vice versa.

Because of their forceful nature, Why's are often "in a hurry" and lack patience. Why's will ask someone a question, and because they tend to answer succinctly, they expect the same in all people. But because Why's are only 9 percent of the population, the answers given by 91 percent of the population are not going be quick enough for the Why. The Why can be impatient to the point, that any question not immediately answered with a quick and decisive "yes" or "no" becomes an irritant to them.

With a belief that no one can do a job as well or as efficiently as they can, the Why is often a poor delegator. This also results in the Why failing to share information.

The Why is comfortable, and one might say in their element with crisis management and will, therefore, fail to plan long range, being overconfident in their abilities to handle things as they go.

The Why may be too brief when communicating and is often considered "blunt" by their friends and colleagues. The Why's are not offended by assertiveness and will often use one-way communication and be perceived as someone that tells instead of sells.

When it comes to working or living with others the Why can't expect too much too soon from the people around them.

Sanguine / Influencer / Who

The most important question in this personality type's life is "Who?" Relationships are their principle motivators. "Who will I be working, living and playing with?" They can be a bit of a "Raymond" from the old situation comedy "What about Raymond?" Just as the character in the show, the Who can become chronically concerned with the opinions of others and find themselves in somewhat of a comic situation here and there as they try to be everyone's friend.

Who's are generally optimistic and will be most comfortable trying to find the positive in any situation. They will sometimes perceive those who do not look for the positive side to be "too critical."

The Who is usually a popular person. They can be loquacious and work to enlarge their pool of contacts, giving them an ever-larger audience with which to share their stories. Who's will not always allow the complete truth to get in the way of a good story.

Because Who's have learned they are persuasive, they tend to exude self-confidence. This is necessary for the Who, as they like moving in new circles where they are confident they will meet people.

Who's work well on a team and are positive motivators. For this reason, they can generate enthusiasm in project groups.

Who's are flexible, since, in order to meet new people, you must be willing to do new things. The idea of having an adventure, so that they have the story to relate about the adventure, is appealing as well.

The Who is friendly and poised, but may not be organized. Who's know the value of networking and usually leave a business trip, meeting, or convention with a number of business cards. Web applications such as Facebook© are drugs for the Who.

Because they do not like to be perceived as arrogant, Who's will indicate that they do not wish to be recognized, but will often privately find great joy in public recognition, especially from those they love and respect.

Melancholic / Steadfast / When

The primary concern of When's is their future. The When is often considered the "Heart of Gold" personality. They are nurturing and willing to listen. The average When is dependable at work and home and loyal to their friends and family. They are long term workers and prefer career employment to jumping from job to job. They are the same in their familial relationships and will often stay in an unhealthy relationship for long periods hoping that time will sort it out.

The When believes in historical procedures with a "slow and steady wins the race" approach to things. They are fairly balanced, even tempered, and approachable. They can be dogged in their persistence and stubborn when pushed.

When's are hardworking and good at keeping secrets. You can cry on their shoulder and the information will remain within their faithful breast. They are technically proficient and love to be needed, procrastinating when a project nears completion for fear of not being needed anymore.

In appreciating established procedures, When's do not like to be pushed into change they have not had time to consider. They are sociable and not very confrontational. They will be a lifelong friend in word and deed. They have strong private convictions and generally think in terms of "right and wrong."

The When is someone you can turn to when in need, and they will actually jump in and help, especially when it is clear that they are needed.

Phlegmatic / Compliant / What

The What personality is detailed oriented and wants information in abundance to make decisions. The What is cooperative with others, preferring to be a team member, rather than leader. They are accurate in their calculations, as they ensure they have dotted their "i's" and crossed their "t's" before presenting their results.

Because they are careful and cautions people, What's are well-prepared for situations – situations for which they usually spend a great deal of time planning. They do not shop without a list, nor learn of an appointment which they do not put on a calendar.

The word "compliant" has been applied to this personality type by Dr. Steven Rhodes. This refers to the fact that this personality type implements systems, complies to them rigidly, and expects others to do the same.

What's are analytical by nature and monitor the results of their systems. This does not mean that change is easy for them, nor does it mean the system they may implement is the "best" system, but it will be the most comfortable system for them.   They will listen to arguments for a new system, but will debate using logic, as opposed to using what the rest of society refers to as common sense.   For What's, common sense and logic are the same.   For the rest of the world, this is not always the case. Often, common sense might mean it is permissible to violate a small rule or operate in a grey area for greater efficiency or speed. The idea of breaking a rule or not adhering to a standard operating procedure is unheard of to the What.

The What is a bit of a perfectionist. Shoes are lined up, files are filed, and something in writing is far more valuable to a What than something spoken aloud.

If you have read through the personality types and thought there is not one type which applies to you completely, you may be right. Although one is absolutely primary, aspects of the others can be present as well.

In seeking symbology to represent the typology presented above, it could be said that the point within the circle is the perfect symbol of the spiritual man, with the square being the perfect symbol of the material existence.

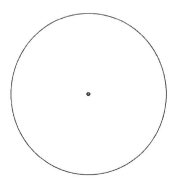

Point Within a Circle

To reconcile or realize the entire spiritual self is to recognize all of our potential, which is all of the personality types combined. So, for an accurate picture of the personalities, the Ego and the Shadow must be part of the equation. In so doing, they show us our shared or collective traits and the converse traits we are likely to lack; in other words, our weaknesses.

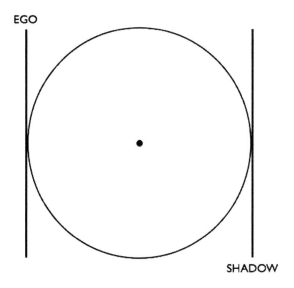

The Point within a Circle with Parallel Lines

So, in trying to illustrate the personality types, a singular symbol has arisen again and again throughout history.

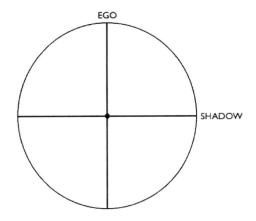

The Point within a Circle with Crossed Lines

The personality types that "touch" or share a line are likely to share traits, as few people find themselves iconic in their type.

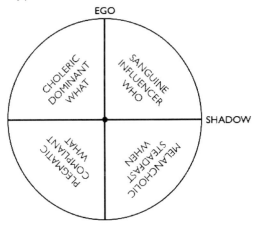

The Point Within the Circle with the Typologies

For example, we are not perfectly a Why or perfectly a Who,, but will likely be a Why with strong Who or What traits or a Who with strong Why or When traits.

For an accurate picture of a person's type, we must take a right triangle and superimpose it toward the point within the circle. The area occupied with the triangle provides the best symbolic representation of the person's type.

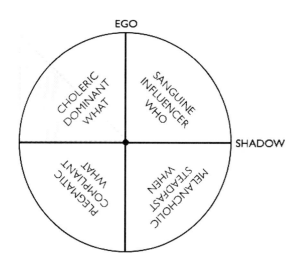

The Point within a Circle with a Right Triangle

Once a person can know himself completely, then he can know others. He can be accepting of his life both materially and spiritually. It might be said that in order to understand what makes a whole man, we must identify the point within the circle and then apply *right angles, horizontals and perpendiculars.*

The person who reconciles themselves completely might be said to have an accurate grasp of the material, the spiritual, their ego, and their shadow.

It is important that once the material and spiritual are reconciled through the recognition of the types, we remember the *place from whence we came.* Where we first stripped ourselves of false ego-driven illusions or were divested of our human defense mechanisms.

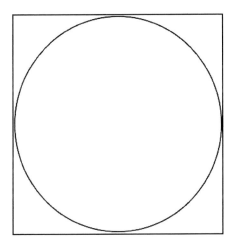

The Squared Circle

These are necessary communications devices in the material, but can cause foolish and dishonest self-evaluations, that result in unrealistic and false self-perceptions. In simpler terms, they become mechanisms by which we lie and then believe those lies.

The symbolic representation for the material man in this world, who remembers these concepts and has reached that Mastery of Self, was drawn by the ancient alchemists who founded Freemasonry as:

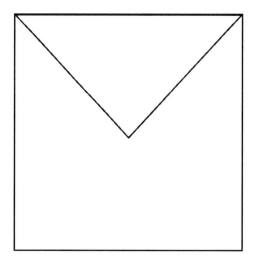

The Apron

The alchemist of the Enlightenment also associated this symbol with Calcination, the application of fire to a substance to achieve a pure white state after it had been broken down to the Caput Mortem or Dead Head.

The apron is aptly assigned as the emblem of a Mason, because it is through the process of the death of our old perceptions and re-birth in honest evaluation, that a man can truly know himself.

This discussion means little, if specific references to the personality types do not exist within the ritual.   If a tenuous connection between the symbols of the lodge and the psychology of self are the only thing I was able to provide then it would be correct to declare this association as a speculative reach and lacking academic viability. For there to be assurance that this hypothesis is valid, we must next evaluate Masonic ritual and any direct correspondence.

Chapter V

Masonic Ritual

Before we discuss Masonic ritual, I believe it is important to provide context for this discussion. There are three things I wish to address prior to entering into this part of the narrative. First, I wish to address the profane who happen upon this book. This book was written for initiates. Yet, I do recognize, when you write a book and make it available to everyone, anyone might end up with a copy. If you are reading this with a healthy curiosity about Masonry and may be contemplating petitioning a lodge, and you are concerned about "spoiling" any of degrees, then I want to warn you: Although I do not discuss anything within these pages related to Masonic ritual which is not appropriate for this forum or which has not previously been presented and discussed at length, I do make direct reference to rituals and degrees of the Craft. Although the manners and forms routinely considered secret are protected within these pages, it is likely that you will discern something of the nature of our practices by reading further. Should you choose to continue, you do so with this knowledge.

Second, I wish to address those who will claim I have gone too far in my narratives. I have printed nothing in these pages which is not already monitorial and has been printed in full and complete language by many different regular Grand Lodges, to include the one to which I am beholden, the Most Worshipful Grand Lodge of Colorado; and which has been printed, referenced, and discussed by many respected Masonic authors and historians.

Finally, I wish to state the following unequivocally: Masonry has had, does, and always will have secrets. Those who believe that Masonry has no secrets are uninformed or have chosen to remain willfully ignorant of the Mysteries of the Craft. The secret that appears to be the most allusive would be finding Masonry practiced in the lives of those who claim membership. The Craft's own philosophies being absent in the labors of its members should not be a one of our secrets.

I will expose nothing which I am obligated not to. If your argument against this presentation is that Masonic ritual should not be discussed outside of a Lodge, I must counter with, were the current relationship between the sublime Mysteries of the Craft and their adherents different, that of actually being practiced in the lives of its members outside of the lodge, then there would be merit to your argument. However, until Masonry recovers its secrets, I believe it is the duty and concern of every Mason to reinvest the Craft with "that of which it has been divested."

The section of Masonic ritual we will start with is often referred to as the Middle Chamber Lecture. In other jurisdictions it is referred to as the Stair Lecture or Junior Warden's Lecture. There are jurisdictions that take the lessons found in the Middle Chamber lecture and insert them elsewhere; still others, sadly, make the Middle Chamber an optional part of the work. Thus, underscoring the disturbing mindset which holds that we must mass-produce Masons, for fear the lodge will wither away without rushing men through, when the reverse is true.

The idea of the Middle Chamber, as part of the metaphysical and psychological experience, dates back to the origins of the Mysteries themselves, including references found in the Judaic mysteries. Mackey recognized this:

> "There were three stories of side chambers built around the Temple on three sixths; what, therefore, is called in the authorized aversion a middle Clamber was really the middle story of those three. The Hebrew word is 'Yatsang.' They are thus described in First Kings vi, 5, 6, 03: And against the wall of the house he built chambers round about, against the walls of the house round about, both of the temple

and of the oracle: and he made chambers round about. The nethermost chamber was five cubits broad and the middle was six cubits broad, and the third was seven cubits broad: for without in the wall of the house he made narrowed rests round about, that the beams should not be fastened in the walls of the house. The door for the middle chamber was in the right side of the house: and they went up with winding stairs into the middle chamber, and out of the middle into the third.

These chambers, after the Temple was completed, served for the accommodation of the priests when upon duty; in them they deposited their vestments and the sacred vessels- But the knowledge of the purpose to which the middle chamber was appropriated while the Temple was in the course of construction, is only preserved in Masonic tradition. This tradition is, however, altogether mythical and symbolical in its character, and belongs to the symbolism of the Winding Stairs."[17]

The Middle Chamber represents the same point in the circle referred to earlier. It is a direct reference to the heart as the seat of the subconscious.

I find it interesting that there are those who lack a definition of Masonry, when within the Middle Chamber lecture, Masonry defines itself, and in doing so, defines the personality types.

Middle Chamber lectures often begin by stating the man must first recognize there are Operative and Speculative aspects to the Craft. This means that there are Material and Spiritual elements to man. The lecture continues with a definition of Speculative Masonry:

> "By Speculative Masonry we learn to subdue the passions, act upon the square, keep a tongue of good report, maintain secrecy and practice charity"

Each element articulated in the definition of Speculative Masonry targets one of the primary weaknesses of each of the major personality types, thus simultaneously identifying the types and pointing out the major typological obstacle to self-improvement.

The CHOLERIC / DOMINANT / WHY as the assertive, almost aggressive personality type must learn to *subdue the passions.*

The Why personality can be unnecessarily aggressive and will sometimes pride themselves on their brutish behavior.

As noted previously, the Why is always in a hurry. He can lack patience to the point where he will ask questions and grow impatient in the middle of the answers. The Why can be prone to compulsive behaviors, such as drinking, gambling, or shopping to excess. The Why can become prey to the "isms" of the world, if they are not careful, such as alcoholism.

The SANGUINE / INFLUENCER / WHO personality, our likable talker, must learn to keep *a tongue of good report and maintain secrecy*. Our Who personality, in a desire to talk, tell stories, and make friends, is prone to "spilling the beans" and to gossip. He can also be the original "forked tongue".

Because the Who places such a high emphasis on their relationships with others, they will often try too hard to impress others, and may become too involved with others or provide them with too much information, in hope of impressing them.

The MELANCHOLIC / STEADFAST / WHEN, in planning for the future, will often place far too much value on the things they have accumulated in their life. For fear of lacking security, and in placing much importance on the value of a hard earned dollar, the When will often lack *charity*. They are loving people and will give of themselves, but do not want to give away their "stuff"; their behavior bordering on covetous.

Although they lack charity in the material world, there is something the When will give away freely, although they don't like to admit it. They will give, or more accurately, get revenge. In contrast to their gentle nature, the When, already patient and secretive, will always hold a grudge and always get revenge. They do not call it holding a grudge, as such an idea does fit with their self image. The When calls it "remembering." They will go so far as to say, "I don't hold a grudge, I just remember", which to the rest of the world, is a grudge.

The When personality has the admirable quality of being secretive, which can make them trustworthy. However, if out of balance, the When needs to be more *charitable*, not only with their material wealth, but with *information* as well. They will often withhold information and share only what they "feel" like sharing. This is likely a human defense mechanism to ensure that they remain needed. In their minds, if they are the only one with a particular piece of information, they are still needed. Because they purposefully withhold information, they end up working alone and seem "too busy" to make progress and complete tasks. The When is involved in every possible association within the Craft. Yet, they the When does not live up to their potential in any of the bodies, being spread to thin.

The PHLEGMATIC / COMPLIANT / WHAT personality is well prepared, but in placing too much emphasis on procedures, systems, and written rules, they do not always use common sense and lack the spontaneity required for *acting upon the square* and for doing the right thing quickly under pressure.

Their life experiences have taught them nothing is perfect. Doubt creeps in and they become slow to trust others, including their Brethren. Again, they fail to act upon the square.

Their fear of making mistakes can slow their progress and they can become lost in the minutia. The What can get so busy counting trees, they lose sight of the beauty of the forest, or that there is a bear in the forest trying to eat them.

The What will often defer decision making to others, becoming a bit of a stumbling block in decision making processes, over-thinking the details and fearing spontaneity.

The What is the most likely to have an unrealistic self-image and will often see themselves as more talkative, popular, and progressive than they really are. This can occasionally make them seem blunt and socially awkward.

The Types in Ritual

It might be argued that the weaknesses of the most ancient recognized personality typologies located within the ritual are a strange coincidence; or, that as Masonry helps all men by the fact that these same weaknesses, common to us all, appear in Masonry's admonitions, possibly proving only that the drafters of the ritual were intuitive or students of human nature.

These hypotheses become more difficult when the other aspects of the same Middle Chamber lecture are presented as ancient insights into the application of the typologies through perfect communication. It could be argued from what is known about the priestcraft, that the reason for their elevation to such a position was that they seemingly knew the future, and were often revered as oracles. I propose that this has to do with the *application* of the knowledge we are discussing here. Once we have succeeded in the charge "know thyself" and "the universe," we must apply this knowledge; we must transition from knowledge to wisdom, from student to teacher. This transition requires communication.

Both the Middle Chamber lectures and the lessons referenced throughout the various Craft degrees contain the same hidden knowledge of application.

The first of these secret teachings are found in the *senses of perception*, or sense of human nature, as they relate to perfected communication.

The Five Senses

> "All we have to believe with is our senses, the tools we use to perceive the world: our sight, our touch, our memory. If they lie to us, then nothing can be trusted. And even if we do not believe, then still we cannot travel in any other way than the road our senses show us; and we must walk that road to the end."
> - *Niel Gaiman*[18]

The five senses have been recognized as significant to the mystical traditions since time immemorial and since the beginning of human consciousness. As a codified, erudite system, the senses were a recognized part of the writings of Aristotle and his disciples. They are addressed and elaborated upon in both *Physics, Metaphysics, Ploitics, De Poetica, and Rhetoric* and the work *De Anima, Parva Naturalia.* Thus, by Aristotle's time, the initiates of philosophy had well recognized the importance of the senses, but had not always recovered the "True Word," or meaning, of their significance.

From the writings of the disciples of Pythagoras, such as Philolaus, and the various schools of thought that he influenced - to include the teachings of Aristotle - we find that Pythagoreans studied the the five senses and recognized intuition as a sixth sense. The teaching that intuition was the sense adapted to finding gnosis more than the others, and almost as allusive as gnosis itself, intuition was much revered. In this teaching, we catch a glimpse of the secret teachings of our own mystical tradition; a clue that there is something sublime and metaphysical to be gained in understanding the five senses of our nature. A whisper from the past that the five senses are a key to additional learning and understanding.

While I have previously presented this point, it bears repeating, given its importance: when one obtains mastery of the secret psychology of Masonry, when the priests of old gained mastery of the secret teachings of the mysteries, the end result was their heightened intuition made them appear as gods and oracles. The proof of this is not in a footnote, but in the number of Deified wise men currently revered or having been revered in the past.

The ritual of Masonry, pulled in part from academic sources, is a complete compendium of the same mystical instruction of the mysteries.

The Five Senses of Human Nature

The following excerpts are some of the many found in the various rituals of Masonry. This particular set was quoted verbatim from *General Ahiman Rezon*, Daniel Sickles, 1868.[19]

Hearing

"Hearing is that sense by which we distinguish sounds, and are capable of enjoying all the agreeable charms of music. By it we are enabled to enjoy the pleasures of society, and reciprocally to communicate to each other our thoughts and intentions—our purposes and desires; and thus our reason is rendered capable of exerting its utmost power and energy. The wise and beneficent Author of Nature intended, by the formation of this sense, that we should be social creatures, and receive the greatest and most important part of our knowledge from social intercourse with each other. For these purposes we are endowed with hearing, that, by a proper exertion of our rational powers, our happiness may be complete.

Seeing

Seeing is that sense by which we distinguish objects, and in an instant of time, without change of place or situation, view armies in battle array, figures of the most stately structures, and all the agreeable variety displayed in the landscape of Nature. By this sense, we find our way on the pathless ocean, traverse the globe of earth, determine its figure and dimensions, and delineate any region or quarter of it. By it we measure the planetary orbs, and make new discoveries in the sphere of the fixed stars. Nay, more, by it we perceive the tempers and dispositions, the passions and affections of our fellow-creatures, when they wish most to conceal them; so that, though the tongue may be taught to lie and dissemble, the countenance will display the hypocrisy to the discerning eye. In fine, the rays of LIGHT which administer to this sense, are the most astonishing parts of the animated creation, and render the eye a peculiar object of admiration. Of all the faculties, SIGHT is the noblest. The structure of the eye, and its appurtenances, evince the admirable contrivance of Nature for performing all its various external and internal motions; while the variety displayed in the eyes of different animals, suited to their several ways of life, clearly demonstrate this organ to be .the master-piece of Nature's works.

Feeling

Feeling is that sense by which we distinguish the different qualities of bodies:—such as heat and cold, hardness and softness, roughness and smoothness, figure, solidity, motion, and extension.

These three senses, Hearing, Seeing and Feeling, are deemed peculiarly essential among Masons.

Smelling

Smelling is that sense by which we distinguish odors, the various kinds of which convey different impressions to the mind. Animal and vegetable bodies, and indeed most other bodies, while exposed to the air, continually send forth effluvia of vast subtility, as well in a state of life and growth, as in the state of fermentation and putrefaction. These effluvia, being drawn into the nostrils along with the air, are the means by which all bodies are distinguished. Hence it is evident, that there is a manifest appearance of design in the great Creator's having planted the organ of smell in the inside of that canal through which the air continually passes in respiration.

Tasting

Tasting enables us to make a proper distinction in the choice of our food. The organ of this sense guards the entrance of the alimentary canal, as that of smelling guards the entrance of the canal for respiration. From the situation of both these organs, it is plain that they were intended by Nature to distinguish wholesome food from that which is nauseous. Every thing that enters into the stomach must undergo the scrutiny of tasting; and by it we are capable of discerning the changes which the same body undergoes in the different compositions of art, cookery, chemistry, pharmacy, etc.

Smelling and tasting are inseparably connected, and it is by the unnatural kind of life men commonly lead in modern society, that these two senses are rendered less fit to perform their natural offices.

The proper use of these five senses enables us to form just and accurate notions of the operations of Nature; and when we reflect on the objects with which our senses are gratified, we become conscious of them, and are enabled to attend to them till they become familiar objects of thought.

On the mind all our knowledge must depend. What, therefore, can be a more proper subject for the investigation of Masons?

To sum up the whole of this transcendent measure of GOD'S bounty to man, we shall add, that Memory, Imagination, Taste, Reasoning, Moral Perception, and all the active powers of the soul, present a vast and boundless field for philosophical disquisition, which far exceeds human inquiry, and are peculiar mysteries, known only to Nature and to Nature's GOD, to whom all are indebted for creation, preservation, and every blessing we enjoy."

Chapter VI

Understanding the Secrets of Perception

Once a person is invested with a realistic personal self-image, he must learn to "communicate" this new understanding to others.   This transition from raw Intellect to Wisdom gives birth to the neophyte, who is then able to see Beauty.   Wisdom transmits the Knowledge, or provides the *working tools*, giving birth to the reality and beauty of our existence, and empowering others with the strength to, likewise, labor for Wisdom of their own.

Of the Five Senses of Human Nature, the three most revered by both Masons and by clinicians of subconscious communications are Hearing, Seeing, and Feeling, as one of these three senses is always the *primary sense* that drives communications.

Dr. Steven Rhodes teaches that approximately 45 percent of society is sight oriented, 45 percent of society is hearing oriented, and 10 percent are feeling or *kinesic* oriented. This primary sense drives not only our abilities to observe, but also our communications phraseology. It has been my experience it defines our language.

The Sight Oriented

This person is visual, as you might imagine. The average sight oriented person says things such as:

- Do you see what I'm saying?
- Just picture it.
- I just can't see him doing that.
- Look, I don't know.
- I finally saw the light.
- I watch out for things like that
- Look out when you go there.
- He didn't look like he wanted to talk.

When sight oriented people get lost while driving, they turn down the radio. Its common for them to listen to the radio or music in the car, but they won't be able to tell you what the last song on the radio was. For them, it is simply back ground noise.

They will come home from work, turn on the television the minute they walk in the door, then walk away from it. They will sort through the mail, only looking at the envelopes until selecting one or two to open, leaving the rest for later. They may get a snack, converse with other members of the family, and then finally *look* at the television. Once they do decide to *watch* television, they will do so to the exclusion of everything else in their surroundings, focusing their primary sense on what it does best; watching to the exclusion of all else. While their children may be fighting and it may even seem as if the house could fall down around them, unless they *see* something to distract them from their current visual activity, they almost have to be yelled at to attract their attention.

In Masonry, when sight oriented people are asked to describe something they remember about lodge, or something which is important to them, they will describe the *beautiful* temple, *watching* perfect floor work, or describe a time they *saw* a man give a perfect lecture. Please note this phrase: A lecture is a verbal exercise, yet they will *watch* him give a lecture, rather than saying they heard a perfect lecture.

When you hand sight oriented people a book, they quickly fan through it to look at all the pages. Sight oriented people often have to go back and re-read material in a book,as they *scan* more than they read. When they do read a book, they visualize the story in their minds as they read much like watching a movie. This imagery can be so strong, should they go and see a movie based on a book they have read, they will get angry if the actors selected for particular roles do not fulfill their mental imagery of how the characters looked when they read their books. "That's not what they looked like" or "that looked nothing like them" will be a complaint that they might make.

The Hearing Oriented

Hearing oriented people are sound oriented. The *Inflection* in a statement is more important to these people than the actual words which are used. Tone, volume, and delivery are primary for hearing oriented people.

The most important thing in hearing oriented people's lives is *silence*. They value having quiet in their lives during certain periods of time and consider it, as the old adage goes, golden.

Hearing oriented people understand what the levers and knobs are for on an equalizer. This is in contrast to sight oriented people who always thought the purchase of an equalizer a waste of money. Sight oriented people *saw* no purpose for the device other than arranging the lit knobs into an interesting patterns – which is *visually appealing*. Sight oriented people are oblivious to the subtle changes in the music this device is capable of producing.

Hearing oriented people appear to read "slower" than the sight oriented people, but not in reality. In practice, hearing oriented people do not have to re-read what they had just covered because they did not scan the document. As they progressed through the text, they heard their own voice reading the words aloud in their head as they read every word.

The hearing oriented person uses phrases and words such as:

- Listen to what I am telling you.
- Did you hear what I said?
- I'm not talking to hear the sound of my own voice?
- No one ever listens to me.
- I feel like I am talking to a wall.
- Did you hear me?
- Man, that sounds like a great idea.
- Did you hear about that new movie coming out?

Hearing oriented people are more likely to listen to talk radio and prefer voice phone calls to e-mails, believing the lack of a voice makes e-mails or text messages impersonal. They might say that they long for the "good old days" when people used to talk with one another.

The Feeling Oriented

Feeling oriented people are kinesically and experientially motivated. The particular emotion evoked in a situation or their personal likes and dislikes drive the decision-making process of feeling oriented people.

Feeling oriented people have moods for everything in life. When they are in the mood for a particular thing or not in a particular mood, it is unlikely you are going to change that mood. One of the things feeling oriented people find annoying, are other people trying to change their moods. They make speedy judgements about people, determining quickly if the person gives them a bad or good *vibe* or *feel* and it is difficult to change their first impression of someone.

The feeling oriented people do not like unsolicited touches, are not a big huggers, and worry a lot about how the environment is affecting their comfort.

The feeling oriented person will use words and phrases such as:

- I don't have a good feeling about this.
- I'm in the mood to go somewhere
- He gives me the creeps
- That place has a great energy to it
- I thought the book was touching
- It seemed really heartfelt when she said it
- I don't think that was sincere

Often, feeling oriented people want to collect different "experiences" in life, but might be apprehensive to jump right in until they get a "good feeling" about the situation.

There is a list of words in Appendix B associated with each of the sensory types, so we can learn to "norm" people based on language. We will discuss further how to determine type, after we understand the result or the outcome that perception has on our approach to communicating.

The Result

What effect does perception have on our daily interactions?

Take, for instance, a person describing a car that has driven past his home. It is a red car moving at a high velocity.

The sight oriented person might say:

> "It went by so fast all I saw was a flash of red, it was like a streak through the air."

> "It was so quick it was like a blur of red paint."

The hearing oriented person might say:

> "The engine on that car was revving like it was going to explode. It was so loud I couldn't hear myself think over the roar."

The feeling oriented person might say:

> "That car was driving so fast I thought it was going to knock me over. I could feel the wind as it passed by. I think it made the ground shake."

Now that we defined the types and the primary senses of perception, we need to discuss how to determine them in a person and how to apply this knowledge in daily life.

Practical Application

So far, we have reviewed personality typologies and senses of perception; yet, how do we determine which type a person might be and what do we do with that information?

Once the phraseology is mastered and the language is given the proper attention, it becomes easy to determine a person's type. As you listen to your friends speak, watch television interviews, and pay attention to people interacting, you will learn to "norm" a person's type. However, if we aspire to the level of the high priests of old, whose intuitive abilities and typology assessments caused them to be revered, we must find a way to implement our Craft quickly, effectively and accurately.

With regard to typology, we can determine type by asking the person two questions directly, or by asking ourselves two questions about a person, based on our observation of that person. Direct questions are best, in that they do not allow for the subjectivity of our personal biases to enter into the evaluation. Nevertheless, it may not always be practical to ask the questions based on the environment or your relationship with the person you wish to norm. If you are in a business meeting with a person and he or she is trying to determine if you will have a business relationship, it is not the time to start asking typological questions.

The questions I prefer to use were developed by Dr. Steven Rhoads[20] for use by law enforcement officers in the high stress environment of an interrogation room. Their effectiveness was so extraordinary in the interrogation room, the method has branched into leadership and relationship training. However, outside these fields, they still work in any setting in which human beings interact using language. Again, you can ask these questions directly, or of yourself, about this particular person.

The Questions

"In general, are you more competitive or more laid back?"

It is important to state "in general" because people sense when they are being normed and they also have a natural distaste of being limited to absolutes. The "in general" terminology removes the absolutist approach and, therefore, removes the argument.

If the person answers "competitive," you should follow up with the following question:

"In general, when you want something done; are you more likely to tell someone to do it or try to persuade them to do it?"

The person who answers:

"Tell," is a Why personality type.

The person who answers:

"Persuade," is a Who personality type.

Now, returning to the original question, "In general, are you more competitive or more laid back?" we will attend to the person who answered "Laid Back":

For this person, you should ask the follow up question:

"In general, would say it's okay to let some things go, or would you say you're a perfectionist?"

The person who answers:

"Let some things go," is a When personality type.

The person who answers:

"Perfectionist," is a What personality type.

This means we can begin to approach this person using phraseology that appeals to the strengths, wants and needs of the identified personality type.

The When personality types will often respond with "it depends" when asked about being competitive or laid back. When you hear "it depends" as an answer to this question, do not get into an argument or lengthy discussion. Follow up as if they answered laid back. If they answer "it depends" again, don't worry. The minute you hear, "it depends" you are likely dealing with a When personality type.

Scenario Examples

You have a major new undertaking for the lodge. The lodge has been having major issues with the building and wants to investigate some ideas for either selling the building or increasing profitability.

Now let's approach this project by asking each of the personality types to "buy in" to the idea of helping with the building and heading up one of the associated programs.

Phraseology for the Why / Dominant personality:

"Hey Paul, the building is facing some major challenges and that's a fact. This is going to be a big job that will need a strong leader who isn't afraid to jump in and get a little dirty working things out. If you are up to the challenge, we must get going on it right away. We need to get some things accomplished and don't have time to sit around talking anymore. We need to be doing!

Notice the key words we used: Major, challenges, facts, big job, strong, leader, working, right away.

We also appealed to the idea this was a crisis and the Why person tends toward crisis management. They enjoy a challenge and hard work, yet sometimes lack patience. We included a need to jump in and move quickly and highlighted the challenges.

Phraseology for the Who / Influencer personality:

"Paul, the lodge family is facing some serious issues. We need a person that is committed to his Brothers and who the Brothers like and trust in return. If you can tap into some of that enthusiasm of yours for Masonry to help spread the word about the project and use some of the contacts you seem to have to help make it happen, I could really use you as my right hand man on this one."

Notice the key words we used: Family, committed, trust, and contacts.

We also appealed to his need for relationships and interactions. We appealed to his having contacts, that he was trusting, and enthusiastic - all completely natural for the Who / Influencer.

Phraseology for the When / Steadfast personality:

"Paul the building has some issues and we are going to have to deal with them soon. It's not something we should jump into headlong, but we need to give it some thought. Once we do, we need dedicated men on what is going to be a long-term project. Determination and steadiness are what's going to win this race, and we need someone who has a vision of the future to help take us to a secure one."

Notice the key words we used: Need, dedicated, long-term, determination, steadiness, vision, and future.

We have appealed to the Brother's desire to be needed, to look toward the future, and to be a part of something that is long-term. We also appealed to his desire not to jump at something to quickly, but to tackle it with dogged determination.

Phraseology for the What / Compliant personality:

"Paul, the building is not doing well numbers-wise. We need to do some in depth research into the numbers and find a plan for saving it or selling it. We do not have enough details to make a logical decision at this point. The Worshipful Master has asked for someone to crunch those numbers, analyze the data and prepare a report. Then after we have a report we need to come up with a system for operating in the black."

Notice the key words we used: Numbers, plan, details, logical, analyze, data, report and system.

We appealed to the Brother's logical and analytical approach to things. Our What / Compliant personality Brethren also enjoy a puzzle and don't mind finding a logical solution to things and assisting in implementing systems.

Chapter VII

Three, Five, and Seven

Having reviewed Typology, Senses, and questions involved in norming people with whom we interact, how do we come back to Masonry and the Mysteries? Are there deeper aspects of these psychological elements in Masonry which can give us a more focused insight?

Hearing the definition of Speculative Masonry we are presented with the numbers of the cube Three, Five and Seven, as we prepare to journey upon the winding stairs. These numbers provide the nuances to effective communication and refer to the communications archetypes. When combined with an understanding of typology and perception we elevate communication to a new level.

The Number Three

The number three is an archetype itself. It is the number we attribute to the divine.

In communications, it is the number by which we lie and by which we persuade. *We lie and persuade in threes.*

The lie is the utmost obstacle to successful interactions; both the lie we tell ourselves and the lie we tell others.

When a person uses three words, three sentences, three commas, three repeats, or three paragraphs, we are dealing with a situation in which they are either trying to persuade us or they are lying to us. It is important to norm the situation to determine the motive of the person with whom we are communicating.

It is not entirely understood in the scientific community why people lie or persuade in threes, but it has been inculcated within our most ancient traditions.

Examine one of the Great Lights in Masonry, the Holy Bible. In Luke: Chapter 22 of the New American Standard Bible,

> "34 Jesus answered, 'I tell you, Peter, before the rooster crows today, you will deny three times that you know me.'"

Jesus then enters a time of devoted prayer in Gethsemane, is visited by angels, and betrayed by Judas. Then the story of Peter continues:

"56 A servant girl saw him seated there in the firelight. She looked closely at him and said, 'This man was with him.'   57 But he denied it. 'Woman, I don't know him,' he said.   58 A little later someone else saw him and said, 'You also are one of them.' 'Man, I am not!' Peter replied. 59 About an hour later another asserted, 'Certainly this fellow was with him, for he is a Galilean.' 60 Peter replied, 'Man, I don't know what you're talking about!   Just as he was speaking, the rooster crowed. 61 The Lord turned and looked straight at Peter. Then Peter remembered the word the Lord had spoken to him: 'Before the rooster crows today, you will disown me three times.' 62 And he went outside and wept bitterly."

One of the most famous lies of history, the denial of Christ by the foundational See of the Church, occurred in threes. As a persuasive element, the number three is found 386 times in the Old and New Testaments combined.

We will examine portions of a modern exchange from an interview conducted June of 1995 on *Primtime ABC* by Diane Sawyer, with Michael Jackson and Lisa Marie Presley, Michael Jackson's wife at the time.

Ms. Sawyer began, *"Did you ever, as this young boy said you did, did you ever sexually engage, fondle, have sexual conduct with this child or any other child?"* Although this topic is difficult for many to discuss, high pressure situations can be excellent tools for evaluation because we feel the need to either persuade or lie at an elevated degree. This statement is not one of scientific certainty, but one of personal evaluation and experience.

When we are under pressure as human beings, we tend to find our best or worst and so it goes with studying human interaction. Find human beings in high stress and the studies become more clear, because we are at our best and worst.

Take Ms. Sawyer's question and break down the elements. When she attempted to determine the criminality of Mr. Jackson's behavior, she resorted to threes, *"engage, fondle, have sexual conduct."* This is significant because she is in a *persuasive* situation: a reporter attempting to gain information.

Mr. Jackson responded, *"Never ever. I could never harm a child or anyone. It's not in my heart. It's not who I am. And it's not what I'm interested...I'm not even interested in that."*

Mr. Jackson broke up his denial in threes. His specific denials are that it's one, not in his heart; two, not who he is; three, that he is not interested in sex.

I am not drawing a conclusion of Mr. Jackson's guilt or innocence, of any particular charge, but when we norm the situation there are a number of alarming elements from a subconscious perspective.

Ms. Sawyer did not ask Jackson if he harmed a child; she asked him if he had sexual contact with one. So the fact that he would not use the same word or words and that his denial is for harm and not sexual contact has deceptive indicators.

Further, another rule concerning communications and threes are the "wouldn't, couldn't and shouldn't" rule.

Honest denials are specific. "No, I did not." When someone provides that they wouldn't, couldn't or shouldn't in the context of a denial, it often means that they already have. What they are really saying is, "I wouldn't do that again, because now I have been caught." Or, "I couldn't do that, because you are watching me now."

Ms. Sawyer asked a common behavioral analysis question, utilized in a number of critical questioning techniques, *"And what do you think should be done to someone who does that?"*

In Western culture, the answer is simple: Punishment. If a person is not constrained by religious beliefs for saying so, the punishment described will usually include mutilation or harm to the genitalia of the offender. "I think you should cut off...."

It is not a difficult question to answer and would take very few words to answer it for most honest people.

Mr. Jackson responded, *"To someone who does that? What do I think should be done? You want to know what I think? Gee, I think they need help in some kind of way, you know?"*

Mr. Jackson asked three questions before answering. Then, he answered with a question by using a communications technique called a "qualifier," designed to bring in and inculcate the listener, "you know?"

Prior to this interview, Mr. Jackson had been contacted by law enforcement who had a court order to take pictures of his genitalia, so that they could use them in a sort of identification with the victim. Mr. Jackson was pulled from his home, taken to the station and forcibly disrobed and photographed nude. This was likely what we might call a life changing experience. Thus, it is unlikely that at the time of the interview that Jackson had any real doubt about Sawyer's next question.

Ms. Sawyer, *"How about the police photographs, though? How was there enough information from this boy about those kinds of things?"*

Mr. Jackson, *"The police photographs?"*

Ms. Sawyer, *"The police photographs."*

Mr. Jackson, *"That they took of me?"*

Ms. Sawyer, *"Yes."*

Mr. Jackson, *"You want to know about those photographs?"*

Ms. Sawyer, *"Yes."*

Mr. Jackson utilized three questions in this exchange prior to providing an answer that, "There was nothing that matched me to those charges."

Mr. Jackson was never convicted of a crime related to this interview, but I will leave it to the reader to decide if he was persuading or deceiving. Regardless of your belief, concerning this man's guilt or innocence this dialog illustrates well that we persuade or lie in threes.

Another common manifestation of the rule of three is when someone denies something by repeating no three times, "No, no, no...don't be silly." You are not being silly and this person is attempting to deceive you.

The Number Five

The number five has three allusions for perfected communication in Masonry. This is why the number five is sometimes pictured in threes upon the tracing board.

The Coffin

The first being *rule of habit*, the second being the *stages of acceptance of an idea*, and the third being *perception*.

Let us first review the rule of habit. We form verbal habits in fives. Once something is repeated five times, we have established the verbal habit by the sixth utterance.

This system of communication technique is highly valuable in communications environments when we are trying to gain someone's assent or consent.

For example, we have studied the personality types and know the When/Steadfast and the What/Compliant personality typologies are often uncomfortable with change. This can be an obstacle in democratic organizations when you take into account that the combined When's and What's make up 70 percent of society. This means a vote for any kind of change in Masonry is likely to meet with resistance and a resounding "no." Any democratic organization is faced with this reality and it is why the most effective businesses are not run as democracies: They simply do not move forward well. While they might prove effective in representation, they do not prove effective in efficient forward progression.

Thus, when we follow the rule of the habitual five, we can assist in overcoming the natural typological resistance to change by allowing for the formation of a habit. The habit can be the perfect cure for fear of change. Returning to our theme of problems with the Lodge building, implementation is as simple as:

"Brethren, I would like to hear from everyone in the lodge. So please do speak up, as I believe that this is an issue that deserves our attention.

We have all seen the issues with the building. Have we not?

We have all heard the problems we are facing with rising costs. Have we not?

We have all experienced the frustrations of making the building sustainable. Have we not?

We would all like to be a part of a successful building, is that correct?

We all want to do the right thing even if we disagree on what this is, isn't that correct?

Can I have your support then for some ideas we have, which might seem a little scary, but we believe will work and help save this building?

All we need to do is present a series of questions designed to illicit a "yes" or "no" response five times in a row. Repetition in fives assists the individual in making this same response a sixth time. However, this approach will not overcome major subconscious objections.

If a man has a strong moral conviction, it is not likely he will simply change this conviction because you have asked him something five times. It will assist in easing typological resistance to change, by making the answer of "yes" or "no" to a particular issue more comfortable on a subconscious level. What we have done is help psychologically place the respondent at ease, not to trick him.

The last of the allusions to the number five in communications is overcoming the natural emotional responses to an issue. In modern times, this was best documented by Dr. Elisabeth Kübler-Ross who introduced them in *On Death and Dying.*[21] Her model was applied to people facing terminal illnesses, but its application is more widespread. Any time a person is facing a stressful decision, this model must be applied. The severity of the stages can simply be adjusted to the situation.[22]

The five emotional stages are:

1. Denial

2. Anger (Toward Others or Blame)

3. Bargaining

4. Depression (Towards Self or Shame)

5. Acceptance

For communications theory, it is best to refer to anger as blame, in that facing the decision-making process, we go through a period when we direct our frustrations outward. This is more accurately termed the blame stage for our purposes. The depression step can, likewise, be more accurately termed the shame stage for our purposes, as the anger is turned inward and we blame ourselves for the situation we are in.[10]

Although our present culture approaches these as psychological periods in the minds growth toward acceptance, they are also communications situations that must be dealt with to obtain agreement, consent, or conscious acceptance. The five stages provide a powerful medium for the communicator and, I believe, were known by the ancient mystics in their growth toward understanding oneself.

The Five Stages and Platonic Solids

The Emotional Stages can be associated with the Platonic Solids in their entirety as follows:

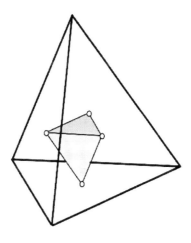

The Tetrahedron

The Tetrahedron as Denial. The vertex configuration of the Tetrahedron is 3.3.3 and its element is Fire. Denial is the Fire of Truth. We must enter this stage as we confront that which is superfluous in subjective perception, and allow it to be burned away. The first stage of initiation into acceptance. Fire.

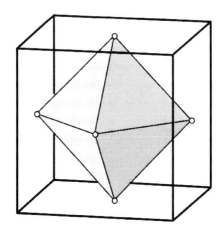

The Cube

The Cube as Blame. The vertex configuration of the Cube is 4.4.4 and is associated with the element of Earth. In this stage, we have descended into ourselves, the material, the Malkuth.

There is a primal aspect to the cube. The rabid dog lashes outward, so to does the man in this stage of emotion. It is savage in its quest to avoid the pain of realization.

This is a bitter search for others in our present material existence to lash out at or point toward. This is a desire to have a physical being and reality to explain away our situation, so that the fact of the matter does not have to be looked at internally, spiritually or subconsciously. This is a primal and outward manifestation. This is the conscious mind doing what the conscious mind does best: look outward.

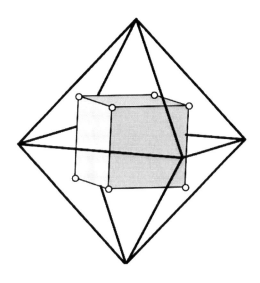

The Octahedron

The Octahedron as Bargaining. The vertex configuration of the Octahedron is 3.3.3.3 and is associated with the element of Air. Just as air is associated with the humor blood and the sanguine associated with compromise for the stability of relationships, so to the Octahedron is with bargaining: "Can't we work this out?"

This is apply middle ground. A strong desire to split the difference between blame and shame. A degree of willingness to take some personal responsibility and acceptance, but a strong rejection of taking "all" of it in, whatever it is.

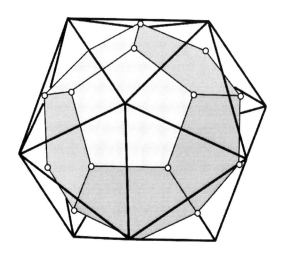

The Icosahedron

Icosahedron as Depression or Shame. The vertex configuration of the Icosahedron is 3.3.3.3.3 and is associated with the element of Water. Aristotle would associate water as cold and wet, similar to the hot and wet of air. Water is creative, but also irrational and can fail to allow for movement. Thus we can drown in indecision. This is the indecision of shame, the recognition that the decision rests with us alone, but so does the obstacle of fear prior to making that decision; the treading of water before deciding to sink or swim.

The Dodecahedron as Acceptance. In Masonry, the esoteric symbol of the dodecahedron is provided as an allusion to this ancient mystical teaching. Its vertex configuration is 5.5.5. and is alluded to in the Scottish Rite symbolic lodges. Its allusion can still be found in the York lodges, but with greater difficulty. The vertex configuration of the Dodecahedron is associated with Aether, Gnosis and the Universe. In Jungian terms we would say the collective unconscious or the constant and universal subconscious. Masonry would refer to it as the highest hill and lowest valley, the terrestrial and astral globes upon the Pillars of the Material and Spiritual man. The Dodecahedron has also been associated with the globe and the vessel, cup or grail. It is realization, acceptance and self awareness.

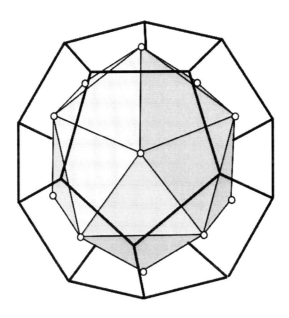

The Dodecahedron

Its worth noting that the Dodecahedron has made its way as a symbol into many of the Masonic systems and into Rosicrucianism. It can also be found in a number of pieces of art from the time of the medieval cathedral builders. A common manifestation for the Dodecahedron is the Gnostic Rose and is found in great frequency in medieval churches. It would make sense that as people sought Gnosis or *accepted* Christ into their lives, they would enter through an archway adorned with the mathematical and archetypal symbol of Acceptance. This is just as the Entered Apprentice begins a journey toward mastery between two globes that conceal the Dodecahedron.

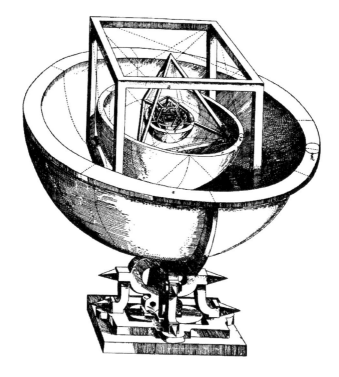

Kepler's Solar System

An argument can be made that simply being exposed to the symbols can speak at an archetypal level to the cosmic Mind, the collective unconscious. I would counter that Masonry is labor, and we must learn, struggle, and reach for improvement in ourselves. A system without labor is a system with no place in Masonry. If simply staring at a symbol is enough then the lie could not exist in the presence of the True Word, and we know that both fight for a place in this world.

The Rose Window of Strasbourg Cathedral

As we have done continually throughout these writings, we will provide examples of real world application for immediate use in the quarry of our daily lives.

For our example, let us imagine that we are approaching a Brother whom we know to be a sight oriented Who/Influencer personality type. For the purposes of this scenario, we will speak to the Brother about subduing his passions and not being confrontational in lodge. In doing so, we will ask him to admit that he has been a source of conflict and consternation in the lodge meetings.

> *"Brother can I speak to you for a moment about some things I have **seen** in lodge? It will just take a moment and I think it is important that we speak because it affects several of the **relationships** with our Brothers.*
>
> *I have had the opportunity to **watch** what has been going on in lodge lately and I have also **seen** how it has affected **those around you.***
>
> *I appreciate your passion, but as we can all appreciate that **we are Brothers**; you are hurting your **friends and Brothers**, and because of your passions, I believe you have been **blinded** to it."*

In these first statements we have appealed to the sight orientation and the typology of our Brother in question and we have addressed that there is a problem.

> *"Now, I know how hard it can be to **see** things from others' perspective, and our first reaction is often to say, 'That's not the case.' But since I am providing a **picture***

> of another Brother's perspective, mine and those I have been sitting with, it would be difficult to **deny** that this isn't what we **perceive**."

We have now addressed the denial phase of emotional acceptance and moved him past it, taking away the argument in terms that appeal to his sight orientation.

> "I can also **see** how it would be easy to get **frustrated** because there have been times when I have **seen** a few of the Brothers push your buttons and I know, likewise, that it is only because you **care** that you are **frustrated** and even a little **angry**. Maybe even a little **angry** at the **exchanges** that have lead to this discussion."

We have now addressed the anger or blame phase and acknowledged that this is normal, and that you can understand how this would be the case, which implies others can understand as well. It is not in bold, but "push your buttons" is a word picture, and all word pictures appeal to sight oriented people and was worked into the language for that purpose.

> "But I think that we can **both** agree that when we **picture** a perfect lodge it is filled with all kinds of Brethren and because we **love our Brothers** finding **balance** is important."

The word "both" has the importance of providing that both the speaker and the listener are in a relationship, and relationships are of primary importance to the Who/Influencer personality; thus, we have been continually appealing to this aspect.   Now, not only are we appealing to his relationship with his Brothers as a whole, we have pulled him into a one-on-one relationship with ourselves.

Balance is synonymous with compromise and bargaining.   It is now time to move toward personal responsibility or the shame stage.

> *"Brother, it can be a little **embarrassing** when we have to step up to the plate and acknowledge that we have made a mistake, but in the end, that is where Masonry really **shines** in a man's life.   When we are a perfect ashlar, we don't need Masonry.   It's when we have fallen a little short, **especially with our Brothers**, that we need Masonry.   Brother when I **look** at you I **see** a good man who has made a **small** mistake, who did something spur of the moment in lodge when passions were rising. But if you can **see** how this has affected **your Brothers**, then I think you can also **see** what we must do Masonically."*

Here we have addressed the embarrassment associated with taking responsibility for our own actions.   Embarrassment is synonymous with shame in this instance.   Small is a word related to size, which is a visual concept so we never forget that we are dealing with a Who/Influencer who is sight oriented.

> *"I think we can both **see** what should happen Brother.   We need to take it down just a notch.   It's not just about how you **feel** or how you **see** it, it's about how **your***

> *Brothers see* it as well. And right now I
> think they need to *see* you subdue your
> passions and might even need to see a bit
> of an *apology* from you as well. I think this
> would *show* the Brothers that you care, that
> you recognize the situation, and that you
> care for them. **Can we agree that we
> should show our Brothers that you care
> and that you are sorry**?"

We close with moving toward an apology, which is a
symbol of acceptance. The Brother has understood
what we were saying, it appealed to his perception and
provided him a journey through the arguments and
obstacles he would normally have gone through on his
own, so that he can arrive at a singular decision of
acceptance with someone.

This is the power of communication. Notice that in
going through the five stages and gaining his assent at
each one, we have also formed a habit of agreement as
discussed earlier.

So that we have a clear picture, let us take the same
situation, but alter our approach for a Brother who is a
Why/Dominant personality typology and hearing
oriented in his perception. We have previously
discussed the Why/Dominant. We know that he is
rational, succinct, and almost a little aggressive in his
style. He is direct and appreciates directness. If we
use too many words we have lost him.

> *"Brother, can I* **speak** *with you privately for
> a minute? I want to* **talk** *with you about a
> situation in lodge that involves you."*

We have used sound oriented words so that we appeal to his perception and we have also answered his first question. He is a Why/Dominant and if we ask the question about talking to him privately without saying "why" we wish to do so, we will slow communication as he asks a number of Why oriented questions.

> *"The Brethren have been upset by your **statements** and the manner in which you present them in lodge. The Brothers **listening** to you said you **sound angry and forceful**."*

The words statement, sound and listening are sound oriented words, designed to appeal to the hearing oriented Brother. Angry and forceful are words that appeal to the Why/Dominant and he understands their meanings. He might not admit this, but he likely prides himself on being forceful and often describes himself as being angry.

> *"I would like to **cut to the chase** here and talk about the real issue. The Brothers **tell** me that you are a leader in this lodge. A Brother they can **talk** to about even the most **difficult** topics."*

Telling the Brother you are getting down to business appeals to him. You have also called him out as a leader, which is something he wants at the core of his desires. You close by telling him that he can be talked to about the most difficult of topics. This further elevates the idea of leadership and a challenge, both strong appeals for this Brother.

*"It will be a **challenge** for you to overcome what is natural to you, **direct** and **assertive speech**. It is **critical** that you handle this like a **leader** and not go and **confront** those who you believe should have **talked** to you about this first. We are **talking** now. That's enough."*

As with the previous example, we are using the typological phraseology that appeals to our Why/Dominant - a more forceful and direct approach than we did with our Who/Influencer Brother. We are also using less words, a dramatically different approach.

*"If you are going to be the kind of Brother they **say** you are, then there is **no compromise** in this. You need to be the man they **talk of and not about**."*

We are not compromising with this Brother, as he sees compromise as wishy washy. So we are saying that the world is as he perceives it. We are saying it, not asking him to see it. This is also important.

"You are not the kind of man to lament and ask a bunch of pity questions.

We are also removing the shame stage by indicating we don't need to waste time with it. Again, we move past this stage by appealing to the manner and form of the personality type.

*"You are a **doer**, so lets **stop talking and start doing**. What do you say, **tone** it down a bit in lodge, but keep that 'get it done' attitude at the same time?"*

With asking him to stop talking, we appeal both to his hearing sense of perception and his typology, which wishes to do things versus talk about them. Tone is a sound based word and again appeals to the sense of perception.

It is hoped, that in viewing, hearing, and experiencing these two different examples, rooted in the same issue, you can begin to play with different combinations and examples. This system only works if you have the courage to try it.

Human beings might enjoy learning, but to take an academic concept from a classroom or a book and implement the idea through action in their lives is very difficult for most. It is why mastery is reserved for a few, as is success.

For many, it is easier to keep our ego intact by calling it, or equating it to, integrity. In this way, we can pretend that we are staying true to ourselves. This is more desirable than knowing ourselves, checking our egos at the door, and moving forward into the world of real change, fulfillment and progression.

The Number Seven

The number seven alludes to Mastery. This Mastery can best be understood in modern terms by applying the seven traditions in communications theory as defined by Robert T. Craig,[23] from the University of Colorado. The traditions defined by Craig are a teaching that permeate the mysteries, although Craig has given them a modern voice. They have been long veiled in Masonry within the Liberal Arts and Sciences.

The current school of communications theory, as a field, would divide the "traditions" as:

- Semiotic
- Rhetorical
- Phenomenological
- Cybernetic
- Socio-Psychological
- Critical
- Cultural

For the purposes of this narrative, the "Masonic" definitions used for the Arts and Sciences originally by Brother William Preston and published so frequently by other Masonic scholars beholden to him for his effort, will be given in *italics* as such:

> *Grammar teaches the proper arrangement of words according to the idiom or dialect of any particular people.*

Grammar is associated with the phenomenological aspect of communications theory. It is the dialog aspect and might also be described as the experiential aspect of communications.

> *Rhetoric teaches us to speak copiously and fluently on any subject. Not merely with propriety alone, but with all the advantages of force and eloquence.*

Rhetoric is associated with the rhetorical aspect of communications theory. It is the art of speaking with fluency.

> *Logic teaches us to guide our reason discretionally in the general knowledge of things and directs our inquiries after truth.*

Logic would be the semiotic aspect of communications theory and allows us to see the truth of unity and connection, and dispel the falsehood of disconnectedness. Ordo ab Chao.

> *Arithmetic teaches the powers and properties of numbers, which are variously affected by letters, tables, figures and instruments.*

Arithmetic would be the cybernetic aspect of communications theory and the mathematical process of complex systems. This is the understanding of the micro and macrocosms, the communicative ability to speak on many levels. It is at this stage that wisdom is achieved, because not only do we possess raw intellect; we are able to communicate it, and intellect is thus transmuted into wisdom.

> *Geometry treats of the powers and properties of magnitudes in general. From a point to a line, from a line to a superficies, from a superfices to a sold. A point is a dimensionless figure or an indivisible part of space. A line is a point continued and a figure of one capacity, namely length. A superficies is a figure of two dimensions, namely length and breadth. A solid is a*

figure of three dimensions, namely length, breadth and thickness.

Geometry would be a critical part of communications theory and relates to what has been described as discursive reflection. Discursive is defined as "fluent and expansive rather than formulaic or abbreviated." This is the Theory and Postulate versus the hard fact of arithmetic, the scientific expression of faith.

> *Music teaches the art of arranging concords, so as to compose delightful harmonies by a mathematical and proportional arrangement of acute, grave, and mixed sounds. It is a language*

Music would be the cultural part of communications theory. This is the recognition of the beauty found in order of things. A special arrangement of vibration, we find beauty that touches the heart in a way that a simple word cannot. This is expression behind the word or beyond it.

> *Astronomy is that divine art, by which we are taught to read the wisdom, strength and beauty of the Almighty Creator, in those sacred pages; the celestial hemisphere. Assisted by astronomy, we can observe the motions, measure the distances, comprehend the magnitudes, and calculate the periods and eclipses of the heavenly bodies. By it we learn the use of the globes, the system of the world, and the preliminary law of nature. While we are employed in the study of this science, we must perceive unparalleled instances of*

wisdom and goodness, and, through the whole creation, trace the glorious Author by his works.

Astronomy would be the Socio-Psychological part of communication theory and speaks to the interactions of things by which we express creative wisdom.

Communications theory seems a bit of an oxymoron. It takes an idea that would seem simple – communicating - and changes it into a mathematical and psychological system, with lengthy terminology like semiotic and cybernetic. "Can't we just say "hello" anymore?" is a reasonable question, when posed with such complex terms for what seems like a simple idea.

What do all these complex terms mean to the average person in everyday life? How were they so important as to find their way into the Craft as part of the Secret Psychology?

The teaching inculcated within the Seven Liberal Arts and Sciences and now referred to as communications field theory can be "calcinated" and reduced to three principle appeals to a person.

The emotional, rational and personal pleas.

These are important because both the Why/Dominant and the What/Compliant personality types are rational personality types. This means they rely heavily on empirical data and like to have facts and details prior to making decisions; they are not necessarily worried about the effect of their decisions on others, with regard to how the decision makes them "feel."

Conversely, the Who/Influencer and When/Steadfast consider how they feel about a decision and the Steadfast will often defer to "it depends" as a reliable statement of their approach.

The personal approach can also be seen as an appeal to the individual and his best interest or self preservation motives.

If we are to appeal to the person to change directions or "talk someone out of" something, these applications are essentially necessary for the process to succeed.

Understanding just a minimal degree of the human mind in a mechanical sense, helps to understand this mechanism and also assist in understanding why duality is found in Masonry. Prior to giving practical examples of the applications, we will break down why the application works.

Chapter VIII

Balance and the Human Brain

The human mind is physically divided into two hemispheres. Thus, duality is not only a psychological conception, it is a physical reality for how the human being operates. The two hemispheres of the brain are often referred to as the *left brain* and the *right brain*. The left side of the brain is often associated with logic, individualized components, calculations, sequences and language as a communications device.

The right side of the brain is associated with "big picture" thinking, grand schemes, images, color, art, music and creativity.

Notice how the Seven Liberal Arts and Sciences act upon both sides of the brain. This is also true of understanding the hidden definition of communications field theory, inculcated within the arts and sciences. They transverse the mind, so that the mind can transcend.

The symbolic operation of the mind upon both Hemispheres is acted out in lodge during the floor work of initiation which has both communications-oriented and astrologically-oriented allusions. These are not mutually exclusive as the mind, being the microcosm of the Universe, is ruled by the same laws and obligations drawn upon those sacred pages of the celestial hemisphere. It is interesting to note that the celestial hemisphere appears as such from a particular perspective; on earth we observe it one way, from another planetary perspective, another. This would mean *as above, so below*. The idea of a celestial hemisphere exists from the perspective of material solidity, not from the more accurate reality of being a part of that same hemisphere. This is the reality of duality: that it exists in a time and place as a material reality. But there also exists a perspective not available to all that would allow these same things to appear unified. Both perspectives are accurate and real. Just as the ideas and concepts that separate the hemispheres of the brain create a whole mind, so too, the terrestrial and celestial hemispheres form the universe, and by extension, form the man.

The lodge is a layout of man, both mind and body. Brother Kirk MacNulty[1] has well documented the idea of Jungian Psychology as it relates to the layout of the lodge and the positions of the officers. This can be taken a step further, as it is also the physical operation, the operative mind in action or labor, which is why we say that Masonry is labor.

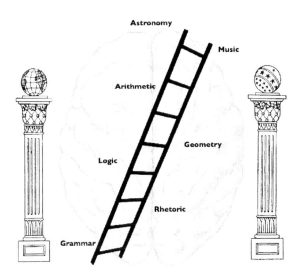

As the neophyte enters the lodge he is a thought, a concept, a spirit. He is being born into existence, or being manifested by the Mind of the lodge. He is *Adam Kadmon* pre-manifest until his raising into manifestation in the material.

The hemispheres of the brain are connected by the corpus callosum or "tough body" of the mind. The three principle aspects in the connectivity between the hemispheres are called the anterior, posterior, and hippocampal commissures. It is important and no coincidence that there are three. These commissures conduct information, thoughts, and ideas between the two hemispheres to coordinate belief and function. This makeup of the brain is often referred to as the architecture of the brain.

The neophyte, or thought, enters the mind of the lodge and is conducted to all three commissures of the mind in forming into manifestation.

The anterior commissure is also called the white matter and connects the two hemispheres of the brain across what is called the midline and is near the front of the *columns* of the fornix. It is *linear* in its makeup. The anterior commissure plays a role in sexuality or Beauty and is represented by the Junior Warden in the South.

The hippocampal commissure is also called the triangular harp and is not well developed in human beings. It has been associated with some seizures, trance-like states, and our evolution from primates. It is strength, raw and pure, good for some things, and obstacle to others. It is associated with the Senior Warden in the West.

The posterior commissure is a band of fibers associated with gray matter and is *circular*. It is found crossing the middle line on the dorsal aspect of the upper end of the cerebral aqueduct. It is strongly associated with pupillary light reflex. This is a reflex involved in how the eye adapts to varying degrees of *darkness and light*.

The posterior commissure is associated with the Worshipful Master in the East, in that, it has the understanding of darkness and light, or balance. It is the white and black of the mosaic together which from a distance is the gray of mutual understanding.[2]

The candidate conducted past the stations of the lodge as he first enters, is being conducted upon the transmitters of the mind. He is being evaluated for all his aspects, physical and spiritual, logical and emotional, or conscious and subconscious.

The candidate is obligated upon the Pineal and Pituitary glands of the lodge. The altar is symbolic of the Pituitary gland. It is found in an area near the top of the spine and base of the skull. It is *a point within a circle* as well. It is involved in the creative process and our growth from infancy to adulthood. The altar is the perfect symbol of the process of birth and growth, the perfect location for this new thought to manifest into the action and labor of being a Freemason.

The Pineal gland is associated with dreams and transcendence. It is represented in the lodge as the Volume of Sacred Law, the seat of morality and faith.

After the obligation upon the material growth of humanity, the altar, and the spiritual growth of the man, the Volume of Sacred Law, the neophyte is given a due guard, sign, token and password of his respective degrees and proves himself as Mason through salutations at the various stations of the lodge.

This is the thought prior to being manifested, passing between the various commissures, through the hemispheres of rational and emotional thought to ensure that the thought is well balanced and formed before being manifested. This is the lodge "thinking" before it acts. The action will be the candidate's release into the profane world outside the lodge. He will pass through the door, guarded by the tyler whose Sword is representative of the tongue, as the door is the mouth, the mechanism of the utterance to the outside world.

As it is said in Proverbs 16:1, "The plans of the heart belong to man, but the answer of the tongue is from the Lord."

The work of man is accomplished in the lodge; the work of God is accomplished when we usher the utterance into the world. Again, the allusion is to the first creative act, the prima force of labor, or the Word. The neophyte is the Word of the Mind.

There are those who will argue that the sword is not an apt symbol for a loving tongue, but it is. They will cite those religious and biblical verses warning that the tongue is a sword capable of issuing forth bitter speech, and this it is. This is when the tongue acts alone or when the heart is corrupt. The sword is a tool of destruction and a weapon of peace all at once.

Application

The application of this esoteric information occurs, as alluded to earlier, in three phases.

When making an appeal, we can do so in such a way as to touch upon the emotional, the rational, and the personal level. The last is an appeal to the ego, or what the person believes to be the case. The terminology of personal refers to the old ideas of the persona, or mask, and its symbol in Masonry is the hoodwink. We will discuss the hoodwink in more detail after providing a practical application of approach for the ideas already presented.

I like to choose everyday examples a man could be faced with, so the secrets of communication and the secret psychology of Masonry can be used in daily living, not put upon an upper shelf and taken out for lodge days like a dusty tuxedo jacket. The secret psychology of Masonry can be worn in our lives as a constant, just as much as morality shouldn't be pulled out and worn with our Sunday church clothes.

The example we will use is that of a Brother trying to convince a fellow Brother that he should not drink and drive. The three appeals should be combined with strong kinesic, that is to say, non-verbal body language symbols. Combined with strong body language, the appeals are most likely to strike a chord, while harkening back to our original hidden teachings within the Seven Liberal Arts and Sciences.

The Emotional Appeal

This appeal will be soft and focus on the part of the Brother that interacts and engages his fellow man.

"Brother I am sure that we can all agree that driving right now, at this moment, isn't the only way to handle this. Isn't there any way we can come up with a better plan?"

Another emotional appeal would be:

"Brother I know you would like to drive right now, but several of the Brothers are concerned. Is there a reason that you can't allow them to feel like they are being Brotherly and allow them to enjoy your company while they drive you home?"

This method combines several emotional appeals and a powerful method that draws upon our dual nature called the "Double Bind Question".[26]

The human mind does not truly have limitless choices immediately available at the moment a question is posed. In order to more quickly assess the situation and provide an answer, which the brain feels compelled to do, it limits choices through a series of "due guards" and "signs" to create the reasonable response. When we are able to construct a question that automatically appeals to the idea of limited choice, but in giving a choice, likewise appeals to free will, we have a powerful combination.

The question we used implies that there is only the choice of hurting our Brothers or allowing them to feel good.

One choice is the "good" or emotionally positive choice. The second is the "bad" or emotionally negative choice.

Other examples of the Double Bind Question include (these are extreme examples so that they stand out):

Have you stopped hitting your wife?

Are you still a criminal?

Have you finally decided to make good choices?

The pairing of body language with these situations should be soft body language.

The Master Mason's grand hailing sign of distress alludes to the power of kinesic communications and provides a hint to the power of non-verbal communication.

It would be good to display the palms during an emotional display, at above waist level, and move your hands way from your body in a shrugging motion.

The Emotional Plea

From a subconscious communications perspective, hand motions below the waist are considered insincere and should be avoided. That is why we hold the hands at about chest level.

The Rational Plea

The rational Plea is one that touches upon logic. It is a fact oriented appeal and comes across harsher and more direct. This is designed as a second appeal. For the purposes of this book, we remain talking with the same Brother to convince him that he should not drink and drive.

"Brother, there is not a single smart reason for you to drive. If your Brothers are concerned for you and have asked to drive you home, there is not a single logical reason to refuse. Let's be smart and get in my car."

The body language that should accompany the rational plea is more direct than the emotional plea, but still not as forceful as we will see in the personal plea.

We should keep our hands open, palms up, bring them to the center of the body at about the level of the solar plexus placing one hand upright in the palm of the other as we make eye contact.

The Rational Plea

The Personal Plea

This is a last chance plea that is forceful and tries, through directness, to break down the ego for reconsideration of the other pleas. This is an on the spot kind of plea.

"Brother is there anything I can do or say to help you make the right decision on your own?"

This plea implies that there is not truly freewill. You are asking the Brother to "save face," or save ego, before he is forced into a decision that others believe to be right.

The Personal Plea

The body language for this is a direct and forceful kinesic motion. You should grasp both hands without interlocking your fingers, but pressing both palms together.

Raise your hands to a full chest level or slightly above. The eyes should narrow and your gaze should be direct.

After the personal plea, we need to be prepared to take some level of action. That action might be to walk away. Or, in the case of our Brother who may have had too much to drink, to step in front him, put your arm around him, explain to him that you love him, and tell him he is not going anywhere.

Chapter IX

The Symbols of Psychology in Ritual

It is believed that up to 65 percent of all communication is nonverbal.[15]   It would stand to reason that, if Masonry contains a secret psychology of communication, then some of the movements, manners and forms within the lodge and the Craft must also contain this teaching.   They do.   They speak to the origins of subconscious and understanding the ego.

The Chamber of Reflection and Hoodwink

The hoodwink is the first psychological symbol in Masonry. The Chamber of Reflection is a dynamic symbol of the subconscious and perception. Together they speak to the condition of mankind.

Rectified, Observant and Scottish Rite styled lodges in the Americas commonly use Chambers of Reflection. It is also a common symbol in Knight's Templar degrees throughout the world. It is and always was part of the Swedish Rite system found throughout Europe. The Swedish Rite system, although open only to Christians, is one of the most fluid, philosophical and potently psychological Masonic systems available. Let us discuss the Chamber in fashion and function, and then we will discuss the symbolism.

The following description would be a common and recognized way of conducting a Chamber of Reflection. The elements within the chamber are provided for a specific meditative or contemplative purpose and there is no part of a Chamber of Reflection that should be done for the effect alone; nor should the Chamber of Reflection be used or conducted in such a way as to instill some kind of juvenile fear in the candidate.

There are descriptions of the Chamber given by Pike, by various Commanderies, and a number of Masonic and esoteric writings. They remain fairly consistent. The following is a description that is similar to most, is in keeping with tradition, and provided by the Grand Lodge of Colorado when a lodge seeking implementation of the Chamber is seeking guidance:

"The Chamber itself should be a small and dark room. Windows should be completely darkened out or covered so as to eliminate all light. This is done so that the candidate will focus on the singular light source mentioned later.

There should be a desk or table in the room suitable for writing. A stool is best so that the candidate must sit up and is unable to slouch or conduct himself in sloth. The Chamber is labor, as is all of Masonry. Black or dark colored furniture can help blend in the room and assist in avoiding distractions.

A mirror should be positioned within the room that the candidate might look upon his own image while he reflects upon his past and contemplates his future.

The Following Should Be Set Upon The Desk Or Table:

A single candle should sit upon the table or desk of suitable lighting to allow the candidate to fill out the questions accompanying this packet. (More on the questions later.)

An hourglass. This will be used to remind the candidate that time passes regardless of our desire to slow it. It reminds us that our time is fleeting and our work upon the earth is important. It is, likewise, a symbol of Masonry and a true hourglass should be used to keep time in the Chamber.

A skull and crossbones. Authenticity is its own reward. Comical or patently false replicas should be avoided. The skull is a reminder of death and transition as both are reinforced in the Chamber. The crossbones are also a hint at the pillars, the porch or portico of man upon which he must stand as he labors in the quarry. The skull is the material trapping of the mind and thought of man, both necessary for existence of freewill, and a necessary component of Masonry.

A small dish of bread. It reminds us of nourishment and sustenance.

A small container of water as a symbol of purity and refreshment. It is also one of the four elements so important within the ancient mystical traditions.

A small container of salt. This component has multiple meanings. Salt preserves and spoils depending upon its use, much like our passions. It also eludes to the soul in an alchemical sense.

A small container of sulfur. This is the third alchemical component to all things.

The following should be in the room or upon the wall:

A scythe, as a reminder of time and death. This symbol is seen elsewhere in Masonry; in the Master Mason degree to remind us of the same thing.

A rooster, such as might be painted upon the wall as a symbol of Mercury. The chemical or alchemical symbol for mercury would prove adequate as well. Mercury is the active element in joining the dualistic principles of man and the Universe. This is the candidate at the doorway to the mysteries who will later understand the gentle guiding principle of mercury within. Mercury, salt, and sulfur also, together, allude to the makeup of man and all substances.

The acronym V.I.T.R.I.O.L., which alludes to *"Visita Interioraterrae, Rectificandoque Invenies Occultum Lapidem."* Translated this statement means, "Visit the interior of the earth, and rectifying it, you will find the hidden stone." This alludes to the philosopher's stone or the perfect ashlar.

Vigilance and Perseverance should be written in the Chamber. We recommend the use of chalk or white paint. Both will be needed to succeed in self-improvement.

Utilization Of The Chamber

Prior to entering the facility the candidate is hoodwinked. Some lodges pick the candidate up at his home and drive in silence to lodge with the candidate hoodwinked as a time of quiet reflection.

The candidate is brought to the door of the Chamber and the first part of the admonition is read.

If the candidate agrees, he is shown into the Chamber and the second part of the admonition is read. The door is closed and the candidate, per the instructions in the admonition, removes his hoodwink and begins answering the questions.

After an hour (you can adjust time as needed, but this is not a rushed situation and doing so is wrong) the Expert or other Brother put in charge of handling the Chamber will retrieve the questions. They might not be completed. This is okay and they should be retrieved when you are ready for them, completed or not.

The Brother who has retrieved the questions enters lodge in the normal fashion and requests permission from the Worshipful Master to read them aloud. The questions are read to the assembled Brothers.

If some new insight or truth is gained by reading the questions, normal parliamentary procedure, as spelled out in the Constitutions, should be followed.

A thorough study of the 18th Degree of the Scottish Rite, the Order of the Temple in the York Rite, and standard Masonic practices in Europe and in Colonial America will also aid in shedding "light" upon the subject.

There are some definite "do not's" when it comes to operating a Chamber of Reflection in the State of Colorado. Do not alter the actual lodge ritual in any way, shape or form. The Chamber of Reflection is a separate activity and can be done outside of the lodge room, or prior to lodge being opened to avoid any conflicts.

You should not add elements to the Chamber of Reflection simply because they are spooky or scary. The Chamber of Reflection is not a gimmick and should not be treated as some sort of comical element nor should it be used as a chance to scare the initiate."

I believe that Colorado does a fine job at its recommendations for the Chamber, but the power of the chamber and its deep symbolism go further."

It is often stated that because the initiation can be seen as a simple of rebirth, that the Chamber is, therefore, a symbol of death. This is accurate to a point. What the Chamber is not, however, is a symbol of the death of the material self.

This statement is utterly ridiculous while we live in this material sphere of existence. To disprove the statement that a man has transcended the material, you need only to watch him eat, sleep, or use the toilet to realize that he has transcended nothing. Cut his left breast and he still bleeds.

If Masonry is designed for man to transcend material existence it has failed worse than first appearances would suggest. It is bad enough that it has often become a beer and pizza club, without the beer; it would be worse if we were supposed to be moving men past the material existence without facing mass murder charges.

What we are changing is the way a man approaches an idea, his perception of it, and not his material self. To be dead to the world or to shun the material world is an out of balance of approach. What the Mason is intended to learn is how to engage his world in a whole new way. Truly speaking the language of humanity at a typological and perceptual level. Speaking to and with them. Not shunning them for a world which is yet to come and must be taken on faith alone.

The removal of the hoodwink during ritual is the removal of the false perceptions driven by ego. This symbol is more pronounced in Scottish Rite Masonry, where it is paired with an entire sackcloth and the candidate is told that he is literally removing superstition from his life.

The power of subjective perspectives can be consuming and one of the greater obstacles to effective engagement with society.

It is fitting then, that the first symbol of our present condition of ego driven communication be removed in the Chamber of Reflection and/or at the receiving of light.

An exercise in the power of subjective thought will likely prove more valuable than paragraph explanations of the same.

Please read the following:

GODISNOWHERE

There are several people who have read, "God is nowhere." The letters, sequence, and phrase are all grammatically correct. They could pass a lie detector if asked, "What did the letters spell out?" and answering, "God is nowhere."

There is another group that read, "God is now here." They are equally correct in that the words spell either statement.

The interesting part is how completely different the messages are. One being one of hope and spirituality and the other being more atheistic.

Taking another example:

WOMAN

WITH

OUT

HER

MAN

IS

NOTHING

Some have read this as, "Woman without her man...is nothing."

But there is a group that have read, "Woman, without her.....man is nothing."

In one reading, women are reduced to nothing. In the other, men are reduced to nothing. Yet the words remain the same.

How many times in our lives have we seen, heard, or experienced something we just knew with our whole hearts how right we were. Maybe we would even be willing to bet a little money on our correctness; there was simply no other way of approaching this particular thing. How many of us only heard one saying in our minds or saw the words in a particular way until the other was presented? Most of us, if we are being honest only perceived one way of reading the words and phrases presented; until the other way was revealed. Masonry is a revealing of new perceptions.

What drives our subjective perception is our ego more than our environment. The environment assists in training the ego, but the ego becomes the filter. When we are not honest with ourselves or become excessively involved in "being right," then we lose an opportunity to gain additional perspective.

The hoodwink is the symbol of the way we used to look at things. Masonry cannot change the physical make up of the man when it seeks to make good men better, but it can assist the man in changing the way the man attempts to interact with his world. The beginning of this new perspective is the shedding of the ego and our subjective perceptions.

There is a school of thought that the hoodwink is about letting go of control. This is partially correct, but in Masonry you never give control over to others. You may surrender yourself up to God in finding new insights into yourself, but you will never give up control. You may give up the perception of it, but you remain in control of your conscious thought and your subconscious.

In lodges not utilizing the Chamber of Reflection, there is still a hoodwink. The bringing of the candidate to light is simply a continuation of the shedding of these older perceptions. We later tell the candidate that he has only begun the journey and his new perceptions are not simultaneous with his initiation; but as his journey continues, he continues to gain insights if he chooses to journey "regularly."

Divesting

The removal of the metallic substances stems from the same teachings of the Seven Liberal Arts and Sciences.

As we begin to undergo a trial of both the emotional and rational hemispheres of thought, we must, likewise, overcome the natural human defense mechanisms. We are not simply pulling off belt buckles and emptying the pockets of loose change. We are ridding ourselves of particular metals and their passive and active impulses that result in the human defense mechanisms. We are ridding ourselves of the common human defense mechanisms that break down honest communication.

The metals were picked as a symbol because they are related to the planets and, later, the Seven Liberal Arts and Sciences.

Gold is ruled by the Sun and relates to raw intellect, the power in force. In its positive roles, it drives change, creation, and leadership. In its negatives, it fails to find value in the opinions of others. The defense mechanisms that arise from gold are arrogance and narcissism. In verbal communication a person might refer to themselves in the third person when using this defense. Bob might say, "Hey Bob wouldn't do that kind of thing." The proper response is to say, "Bob" and simply repeat the name forcing the person off the mechanism and toward honest communications.

Silver is ruled by the Moon and relates to our subconscious reactions. In its positives, it is subtle, caring, nurturing and wise. In its negative aspects, it is dishonest, deceitful, and lacks momentum. This represents the human defense mechanism of passive aggression and denial avoidance. Passive aggression might sound like, "Well, if you are so smart, why don't you tell me?" The response should redirect the aggression to a question that brings the discussion back on point. "Is there any reason we can't simply discuss the topic without getting aggressive even if its hidden or veiled? Is there any reason you can't just be honest?" Denial avoidance is as it sounds, outright denial in the face of overwhelming empirical evidence to the contrary.

Mercury is ruled by Mercury and relates to our use of language. In its positive aspects, Mercury is fun loving, unique, curious, and flexible. In its negative aspects, it's self-centered or, worse, delusional. Mercury represents the human defense mechanism of rationalization and reticence. Reticence as a human defense mechanism can be best described as using too many words to answer the question. For instance, a politician might be asked a yes or no question. "President Clinton, did you have sex with Monica Lewinsky?" "I have not had sexual relations with that woman," demonstrates reticence in answering by using too many words. He could have said, "No." Instead, he provided several words in hopes of masking the real lie. Rationalization is nothing more than offering a justification for the action in hopes of reducing the culpability of the offense. "Everyone takes pens from work, they expect it or they wouldn't buy so many."

Copper is ruled by Venus and relates to love, passion, money and the balancing of polarity. In its positive aspects, copper is conductive and produces balance through education and the seeking of knowledge. At its worst, it is enslaved to passion, vain, and promiscuousness in faith, love and money. The human defense mechanism represented by copper is acting out, which can be described as spontaneous and uncontrolled outburst, without a reasonable concern of the consequences. Acting out can lead to violence and it is best not to confront violent people. But if you must handle a minor episode of someone acting out, it is best to approach it with absolute calmness. Say to the person, "When you are done, I would like to get back on point and finish the conversation."

Iron is ruled by Mars and relates to anger and action. In its positive aspects it is forceful, direct, and accomplishes things. It can overcome difficult odds and reach goals. It is the aspect that allows a man to cut off his own arm to survive a hiking accident where he became trapped or empowers a mother to lift a vehicle off her child when its trapped. In its negative aspects it is violent, uncontrolled anger and rash decision making. It is explosive and harmful. It is related to the human defense mechanism reaction formation. It might be expected that acting out would be the defense mechanism represented by iron, but the person who immediately explodes does not retain the pressure and potency of the one who holds it in for a period of time. This is a more dangerous and destructive mechanism. In reaction formation the person represses unacceptable thoughts, feelings, hostility or guilt and develops conscious attitudes and behavior patterns just the opposite of what they wanted to do; saying or doing just the opposite of how they really feel, or act how they believe one would reasonably be expected to act under a given set of circumstances. This is a pressure cooker response and when the show is denied it reacts in the extremes, consuming parts of a person's life. Addictions and compulsions are born in this defense.

Tin is ruled by Jupiter and relates to visions for the future and welfare for the poor; it is given to law and order. In its positive aspects, tin gives rise to social programs that help the truly needy. It is charity. It also looks toward future posterity and respects social order and interaction in a peaceful society without giving into the brutish limits of Lead which is ruled by Saturn. In its negative aspect, it is bullish, brutish, and unbending. It is dogmatic to the extreme. It is associated with the human defense mechanism of splitting. This is an all or nothing defense and gives way to the slippery slope of logical fallacy. In politics, you see this in the extreme all or nothing approaches to the most volatile issues. People convince themselves if one small compromise happens then it can mean the destruction of all they hold dear. In Masonry, you see this when men convince themselves if things do not occur they way they remember them or are comfortable with, then everything they enjoy will be destroyed. It might sound like, "If we allow alcohol after a meeting, we will end up with a bunch of alcoholics." It is best to point out the fallacy of the issue and argue the point with logic.

Lead is ruled by Saturn and relates to realism, limits, and the empirical. It is base, but malleable. It is the essential human condition. In its positives it provides structure, systems and rules. In its negatives it evokes fear, superstition and isolationism. It is associated with lies and dishonesty. The best approach to Lead, is Masonry.

The Step

The Freemason begins his journey upon his left foot and takes an oath kneeling on his left knee. He cradles the Great Light of God's Word with his left hand. He journeys around the altar to his left side. He visits the several stations of the lodge moving to the Master's leftside and ending with the Worshipful Master himself. He enters through a door that is to the left side of the regular door to the lodge as you look at it. He is entering the lodge through the left entryway.

The left is symbolic of the subconscious. The left side of man is associated with the heart, which is the reason the wedding ring is worn on the left hand and the third finger. The heart was the center of the mind, of thought, and of transcendence. This is important to note, as the idea of emotion was believed to be in the stomach area or gut, which is why people indicate that they have a "gut" feeling.

The left is not the weaker side of man. I repeat, because this will be difficult for some Masons to accept; *the left is not the weaker side of man.* The story of how the left being the weak side of man maked it into the ritual is an interesting one. I believe it stems from a misunderstanding and, therefore, mistranslation of words. In the 1200's, the old English word "lyft" meant weak or foolish and became the current English word left. It is my opinion, that during the few hundred years transition when the word could mean one side of man or weak and foolish that "lyft", was interchanged with weak, the word it also meant. By the 1600's or 1700's, ritual explained that it was the weak side of man in Masonry, when in fact, it was the left side period.[27]

Interestingly, the word weak comes from proto-Germanic language with the word "waikwaz," which meant subtle or bendable. Subtle would be a much more accurate statement than the weaker side of man, for it is the subtle or subconscious side of man that enters upon the journey into the mysteries of the Craft.[28]

The exact time and place that the left became firmly entrenched with the subconscious is uncertain, but it was firmly established in enlightenment era Europe when Speculative Masonry was becoming the society that we would easily recognize today.

This is evident in symbolism of the tarot deck in use as early as the 1400's. An argument can be made the teaching is more ancient. It is likely that the tarot deck received its name from the *tarocchi* decks, which, in turn received their symbolism from Egypt.

Nonetheless, the idea of the traitor or hanged man was nothing more than a symbol of the same idea, the left as a symbol of the subconscious.

The Traitor

This is a powerful symbol in its own right. The traitor always ushers in change. One man's traitor is always another man's hero. He hangs upside down from his left leg, concealing his right, indicative of the idea that the journey of enlightenment and self-awareness is one that must be undertaken with the subconscious. Also of interest, the image used in this book is taken from the Pythagorean Tarot and has, upon its chest, an interesting cut as well.[29]

The alchemical symbol for lead, the astrological symbol for Saturn, and the astrological symbol for Jupiter all share allusions that it is the subconscious aspects of man that the journey to transmutation or enlightenment must be undertaken with the subconscious or the symbolic left side. Initiation is not a conscious activity, it is a subconscious activity when it is done properly.

Lead, Jupiter, and Saturn

Initiation is squarely rooted in the subconscious, as the subconscious cannot lie. It always leaks the truth of the situation. It is within the subconscious that true self knowledge can be obtained. If we can tap into our own subconscious, then we can no longer lie to ourselves. When we are honest with ourselves, it becomes difficult for us to lie to ourselves about others or for the lies of others to touch us the way they once did.

The subconscious is not time aware. The subconscious does not engage in concepts such as real or false. It accepts all things past, present, and maybe even future as occurring in a constant. When the words of a man lie, the 65 percent of his communication that is born in the subconscious tells the truth regardless of his conscious desires to conceal the truth.

We are initiated into our own subconscious. When we do, we find truth. Initiation is always of our own freewill and accord, because it is our conscious will with which we must contend.

A small exercise to assist us in understanding the subconscious is in order.

Read the following sentence quickly. Don't take more than 15 seconds or so and count the "F's" used in the sentence.

FINISHED FILES ARE THE RE-
SULT OF YEARS OF SCIENTIFIC
STUDY COMBINED WITH
THE EXPERIENCE OF YEARS.

Most people find that there are three "F's" when, in fact , there are six.

We consciously decided that "F's" have the sound "eff" and the "F's" associated with the word "of" have a "v" sound. So, we consciously ignore them because this isn't what we wanted or expected. Nonetheless, our subconscious recognized that the answer was not correct and started to search out the truth with a nagging feeling that we were missing something.

When we remove the ego filter from our perceptions then we can be as Jung surmised, comfortable with ourselves, our moods, and our transitions. We can be honest.

Cutting the Chest

The bloodletting of the chest has multiple meanings from a communications standpoint. All of the allusions are powerful and necessary for effective self-awareness.

The idea of consequence is a lost part of our culture today, but a very necessary part of honesty and honest communication. Masonry, however, is older than our current entitlement society, and the concept of consequence might be even more vital for us as a species now than it was when speculative Masonry adopted this esoteric teaching of the mystical traditions.

From a rudimentary point of view, the Why/Dominant personality type respects and needs a shock and fear of sanction for transition from falsehood to truth. Fear of sanction is a fancy way of saying consequences.

From a cultural standpoint, one of the most dangerous obstacles to honesty is entitlement. When a person or group allow themselves to become convinced they deserve something, then they can no longer be honest about their actions. Instead of failing to obtain a goal because we have not labored toward it, we can sit and sob that we have been denied something that was ours.

It could be that Masonry has played different roles in different societies at different times. It may have assisted in promoting the ideas of the Protestant Reformation in one society at one time, and then helped to usher in the American and French Revolutions in another. Different roles at different times.

It could be within the realm of possibility, in a world of technology, self esteem grading systems, texting, violence desensitizing video games, and an overall lack of human interaction and communication that Masonry is to usher in the ancient art of talking to one another effectively, transmitting ideas well, and receiving them without anger and prejudice.

There is a place for some discussion of the detrimental effects of placing the ego before honesty and the obstacles it creates.

Self esteem became the mantra of the entitlement establishment in the 1970's. In California schools, it became common to institute programs that removed grades or, at a minimum, the grade of "F" because of what the idea of failure might do to the young psyche. [19] These same programs, although proven failures as far as measurable growth and achievement are concerned, have cropped up as recently as 2005 in the United Kingdom as they discussed removing "failure" from the public education system.[30]

The result of telling children that everything is okay and the quality of their work doesn't matter are young adult who believe things should be given to him for the sole purpose of ensuring they do not feel bad. Feeling good becomes reason enough. These adults have entered into an American Culture where people don't vote and demand more and more personal wealth without taking personal responsibility.

Many demand the right to be different, but demand that nobody notices. Many bellow the call of freedom, stating that they demand personal freedoms and their inalienable rights, but cry foul when there is a price for their action or inaction. What is really being said is that they want the option to make choices in a vacuum, so that there are no real consequences for their choices. I want want freedom--sort of. I want choice with no consequence; I want decision-making authority, but with the caveat I always get a second chance.

Consequences do not feel good, so I should not have to suffer them, right?

Masonry teaches that there are consequences for your actions, words and thoughts. "May all of our thoughts, words and actions be in accordance with our professions as Masons."

In addition to the piercing which occurs at the entryway, there are repeated requests to hear from the neophyte, in his own words, that he is taking this journey both of his own freewill and his own accord. Accord comes from the vulgar Latin *accordāre*, the translation of which is "heart to heart." This is to say, it is a thought out decision from one educated and thinking man to another. Remember, the heart is the seat of the intellect in the ancient mystical traditions.

The location of the piercing is symbolic of the opening of the mind or intellect to that which was previously concealed. It is for this reason the neophyte will kneel, immediately following the opening of the symbolic mind to the subconscious, and place his faith in the collective unconscious in the form of Deity. This is symbolic of keeping hubris from destroying the journey by allowing the ego to creep in and heal the wound or close the mind. This is why the symbolic dress requires that the chest remain bare.

The reason a square is later presented to the neophyte in a similar fashion, but to the right side, or conscious side of man, is to represent that the candidate can now labor in the conscious world with the knowledge of his subconscious mind. The word square comes from *exquadra* and in later forms of Latin *quadratus*. The two words that form the body of the word are "ex" and "qua" and are of importance to understanding why this implement is picked and why it is of importance throughout the world's mystical, and not so mystical, traditions. The word "ex" in Latin means "out of" or "from within." The word "qua" means "by the route" or "by which route." The meaning for square is, "From the route or path within."[31]

We present the square to the conscious side of man to remind him that, as he moves from silence and learning into labor and action, he must still follow the path within, the one previously exposed; and remind the conscious aspect of man, that the conscience part of him will wish to take over and transition to his old ways as the work becomes difficult. The human species will revert to habit and comfort when forced with the hard labor of working within the realm of the subconscious.

In the Master's degree the Brother is provided a symbol of reunification of the conscious and subconscious aspects of man, because as a Master, he will need to balance between the two using the working tool presented to facilitate this allusion.

The Cable Tow

The locations of the various cable tows are symbolic of the subconscious and communications theory as well. There is little in Masonry that is frivolous. When something frivolous is found, it is usually a modern addition to ritual placed there by men with big egos and little minds that never understood Masonry in the first place. They leave their depressing mark upon it by removing or perverting the truths in ritual which they were never going to grasp in the first place.

The cable tow is meant as a very real physical symbol. At first, it is used to remind us to do the most powerful thing a man can do when learning and when achieving access to the subconscious. To shut up, to be quiet, to remain silent. In communication, the most effective managers and elicitors of information speak only 20 percent of the time after they have achieved Mastery; allowing the person sharing information to speak the other 80 percent. One of the most effective means to find truth from those who do not wish to give it, is to ask an open ended question and follow with a voice vacuum. That is, to remain quiet and stare at the individual with expectation for up to 45 seconds. The dishonest soul hates the sound of silence that the lie causes and the subconscious pushes and screams to force out the truth. The conscious mind fills the void with noise, that noise is usually a voice and that voice carries with it information.

Also, a very simple lesson is this: Put bluntly, when your mouth is moving, your ears are closed and the mind is likely not learning as it should be. The ego will often run the mouth as its motor when it fears that it must learn something, since to learn is to admit that you don't know something.

The cable tow of the first degree is silence and discretion.

Silence may seem a mundane lesson in a world where people's sex lives, financial lives, and personal problems of all sorts are discussed and hashed out among the world's television shows and Internet conduits. The wonderful potentiality of silence is lost in a world of noise. When we keep something in, when we keep secret, when we keep quiet, the energy of that action builds. This is why it is difficult for some, especially the Who/Influencer, to keep silent. But, energy is energy. When we are able to keep things stored within the faithful breast, we can take that stored energy and point it at a productive goal and labor toward it with that stored energy.

In a world with pop psychologists telling everyone to let it out, Masonry teaches the valuable lesson that sometimes you should keep it in.

In the second phase of the Masonic journey the cable tow reminds us to labor with the subconscious, and not the conscious. The presentation at the door to the entrance of the lodge, the cable tow and the position of the obligation are all reminders to labor in the subconscious. For even as we might obligate upon the knee of the conscious side of man, one element of our position points upward towards Deity in a particular shape. Again, a solid reminder to rely on the subconscious as we take upon ourselves the necessity of action.

The final position of the cable tow relates to that old Hermetic maxim, "As above, so below." It is a statement of the duality of man and the necessity to grasp that duality. It alludes to balance within duality , which, when understood, creates the actualized man. *Finis Ab Origine Pedet.* The Master has come full circle. He understands his dual nature, does not shun it, but works with it in Mastery to not only labor, but to teach.

The Presentation of the Gauge

We cannot forget in Masonry that there is numerological significance to our ritual.

The ancient Pythagoreans believed that the Divine plan, the power and wisdom of Deity, could be deciphered in the symbolism of the number. Pythagoras believed that each number was an allegory of what he might have called supernatural communication between God and His people or what we might now call the collective unconscious. The significance of the number was more than a simple system of addition, subtraction, or multiplication. It was more than a representation of how much you owned or how much you stood to lose. The number concealed the Divine plan for everyone and everything. It is fair to say that everyone and everything could be understood as a number or system of numbers in the Pythagorean discipline. The only caveat to this being Deity and His emanations. These were represented by the symbols of the monad, or "1," and the duad, or "2," and were not considered numbers. For this reason, the first number of the Pythagorean mystical tradition was three.

Freemasonry has concealed in its esoteric and astute teachings this same sagacious Craft as it relates to human interaction, communication and the subconscious.

Few Brothers who remember, with even limited clarity, the ritual of our Craft would attempt to refute that the number is a principle symbol of every degree. The very symbol of every level of the Craft is a degree, which can be defined as a position on a scale of intensity or amount or quality, in other words, a number.

Without fear of opposition, it can be declared that certain numbers are of extraordinary significance to the Craft: as we have already discussed in detail the power of the three, five, and seven.

This brings us to the number eight. Where, within the Craft, does this symbol make its appearance? What are we told about it? And what does it mean?

I submit to you the 24 inch gauge. More important than the rule itself is the manner in which we are exposed to it. Many Masonic rituals provide some education that the gauge should be viewed by dividing it. More exacting rituals call for the division to occur equally or in threes.

When exposed to an overly simple explanation within ritual, I waste little time in trying to extrapolate a deeper philosophical meaning. The Kabbalist, alchemist, and ancient teachers of the mysteries assigned to the idea of the saving power of Deity a number; usually veiling the numerical value with name where the letters of that name alluded to the hidden numerological value. So in dividing the gauge we find the number is 888.

Jesus the Nazarene possesses this trait in the Greek spelling of his name. Several scholars believe that the Greeks intentionally moved from Yeshua to Jesus in Greek translations to communicate this esoteric truth.

Allow me to explain. Using the ancient Greek Ionic Ciphered Numeral System, each letter of the Greek alphabet is assigned a numerical value. Jesus in Greek is Ιησούς, I H S O U S, or Iota-Eta-Sigma-Omicron-Upsilon-Sigma. The values of the letters are: iota, 10; eta, 8; sigma, 200; omicron, 70; upsilon, 400; sigma, 200. The sum of 10 + 8 + 200 + 70 + 400 + 200 = 888.

So the Entered Apprentice is told, at least allegorically, that he should use Christos or the knowledge and power of the subconscious to rule and govern his day.

Is it a mistake or happenstance that he is later reminded that this same rule and guide might be used to silence and kill him? There is little room in Masonic ritual for coincident or happenstance. Attributing to our profound ritual to anything other than philosophical truth is often the easy way, which is, sadly, the more travelled way. To assume that nothing lies beneath, allows us to proclaim there is no need to dig. Face value is of little merit in allegory, but it is easy and quick.

Albert Pike, in the work now published as *Esoterika*[32], provides that it is no mistake that the gauge is used to deal one of the death blows during the Hiramic legend. Pike provides that word for gauge, or rule, is the same word used for the issuance of an edict by the Pope, which is referred to by the church as a "Papal Rule."

Is it accidental the neophyte first learns recognition of the great truth gnosis should be his rule and guide. He also learns that this same truth, this same understanding can lead to intellectual death when abused or misused? The great recognition that all things share the same source; the idea Deity can save and destroy depending upon its use and perception is clearly a conviction inculcated within the ritual of the Craft for those who would choose to see it.

So in Masonry we are presented the authority to find for ourselves the truth, the tools to look within ourselves for answers, and the dangers of abuse once we are in possession of the True Word.

The Penalties

There are few things in Freemasonry more misunderstood than the penalties.

We spend more time apologizing for them, trying to explain them, or pretending they don't exist, than any other part of our ritual.   Yet, they are compelling symbols for the subconscious and communications.

The first penalty is derived from two sources. It is both a metaphor for the first stage of alchemy and the first stage of effective communications.

The first stage of spagyric or herbal alchemy requires the practitioner to harvest an herb by pulling out by its roots.   The herb is then broken down in a solution of spiritous liquor or alcohol. The manner in which this is done is by placing it in a salt or sand bath for temperature control, or the rough sands of a sea one might say. Then the herb is agitated twice a day before being placed back in the sand bath.[33]

The subconscious communications message is clear in the penalties. Once again, we are told to remain silent. The power of silence. Masonic degrees apply their own wisdoms. Important truths are repeated five or more times so that they become habit and calm the conscious fears trying to block access to the subconscious. Masonry does not just teach a method of communication, it inculcates that method within the degrees as a means of instruction. In today's world it is almost shocking to find a thing or group that does what it recommends.

The Fellowcraft's penalty is worked the same way as the first degree penalty. It has both operative alchemical allusions and strong symbolism concerning both communications and the subconscious.

Distillation Apparatus

In operative alchemy, during the distillation phase, the apparatus used is referred to as the temple and the peak of the apparatus is referred to as the pinnacle of the temple. There is also a method by which liquid is collected and vapors are released to the air.[34]

From a subconscious communications standpoint, the penalty contains a strong message and it gives us some insight into the timing of the degrees as they are currently worked. It is likely, in my estimation, that the Speculative Masonry we have come to appreciate was born in Europe over a period of a few hundred years, beginning in the 1300's and solidifying as a completely recognizable system in the 1600's and into the Enlightenment Era. The systems and philosophies are much older in many cases, but I am referring to Symbolic Masonry as we have come to experience it. Much of the degree work we experience was influenced by the Enlightenment. There were two things at work then. A belief that reason and science could usher in a new world order and that the organized church, both Catholic and Protestant, had condemned the world to an intellectual dark age while it busied itself with wars and wealth.

The penalty of the Fellowcraft degree is a symbolic reminder that if we ever violate the philosophies of Masonry as a whole, especially those of freewill and self awareness, we might as well surrender the seat of our intellect and the subconscious to the will of orthodox religion and, therefore, hand over our freewill to whatever is the orthodoxy of the day, as it will change with the winds (air) and the whims of its leaders which is correctly symbolized as carnivorous birds.

It makes some followers of the Craft uncomfortable, but there has always been a tenuous relationship with *organized* religion and Freemasonry. There has never been a conflict with a deep and loving relationship with God and Masonry. But, whenever there has been tyranny, or whenever there is a group that would instruct its adherents what to believe in spite of their reason and intellect; Masonry has been correctly identified by these groups as an enemy. Masonry has always sought to strengthen its adherents by improving their own self awareness and the application of the secret psychology in their daily lives. Masonry has religious aspects, so far as religion can be defined as having a loving and personal relationship with God. Anytime a group has placed itself as intermediary between man and God, the Craft is rightly identified as detrimental to the aims of such a group. Masonry instructs man to know himself. Masonry teaches when man does; he can form honest opinions on his own. It further provides that man must have courage in discerning the truth and should tolerate the opinions of others when their personal truths do not coincide with one another. It allows men to have enough moral courage to recognize that not all men will agree, not all men will read the sentences provided earlier in the book the same way, and that does not make them any less the children of God. It does not exclude them from the altar of enlightenment.

It will come as no surprise to the reader, that the penalty of the third degree contains both an operative alchemical allusion and symbolism pertaining to the subconscious.

The alchemical allusion is to calcination or the burning of the putrefied herb. The herb is applied the extreme heat where it is calcinated, or burned to a white powdery ash. The herb itself, by this time has been turned to a blackish substance that looks quite vile and it takes little imagination to determine why alchemists associated it with feces or bowels.[35]

It is a wonderful symbol with which to be associated.

The subconscious communications allusion relates to the gut as the seat of the subconscious. This is why we say that we have a "gut feeling" or a "gut instinct" or having "guts" to do something. This is very common in the Hebrew tradition and the term may have developed first in Hebrew. For instance, Psalm 40, which is often incorrectly translated, often reads in English:

"I delight to do thy will, O my God: yea, thy law is within my heart."

The word "heart" in Hebrew would be לב. The word that is used in the Psalm when it is written in its original Hebrew is מעה or meyah and should be translated "gut." King David also wrote ותורתך בתוך מעי. Meaning that the Torah was in his gut.

The penalty is indicating that if we trade truth for falsehood after the act of initiation, we are in danger of being "scattered" or crazy. There is ample evidence that this was meant to be taken literally. There is a strong belief found in many of the mystical traditions that if you begin the process of enlightenment and turn back from it, that you can be driven mad.

In the verbal traditions of various esoteric and Masonic orders we learn that Pythagoras warned that to turn back after initiation, was more dangerous than to have never begun the search for truth. We are told that the man who stands upon the precipice of enlightenment is in utter danger of smashing against the rocks of atheism.

Once the truth is known, the neophyte can no longer claim stupidity and lack of information, he must choose ignorance if the truth is not embraced.

Completing the Temple

What do we do with this information when we achieve Mastery or the degree of a Master Mason? What do we do with enlightenment? We change the world, we complete the temple, we live better lives.

> "In every rough ashlar of marble is hidden the perfect cube. One is the symbol (archetype), the other its meaning (thought manifest in action). Allegory, the mother of all dogmas, is the substitution of the impression for the seal, of the shadow for the reality.
>
> The work of God is the book of God. For the letters to appear, there must be two colors on the page. Search and discover. You are also a part of his work. The Book lies open before you, and he has given you reason and faith, whereby to read it. Masonry, like nature, teaches by symbols, whereby the unwise are always in danger of falling into superstition, which is the idolizing of misunderstood symbols. The most monstrous faiths owe their origin to

the ancient and true symbols of the sages..."[24]

We should begin with ourselves.

If we are divested of the obstacles to genuine self assessment, we must be honest with ourselves first. Do not decide what personality type you would like to be and convince yourself of it. Ask the questions given and answer them honestly. Personality typology is not like body weight. You can't "hope" to someday be more of a When/Steadfast and decide that you are such. You cannot change your personality, you can only capitalize on your strengths and minimize your weaknesses. To believe that you should change your personality typology is a poor and misguided approach. There is not one typology better than another. One might be more suited to a particular job or employment over another, but for every place or situation in which one typology excels, there is one where it fails and vice versa.

Practice daily meditation and visualization techniques working on the application of self knowledge in various scenarios. I use the term visualization loosely, in that, sight oriented Brothers will use just that, visualization. But our hearing oriented Brothers will talk themselves through exercises with their mental voice. Kinesically oriented Brothers should feel comfortable doing experiential exercises.

The technique is to pick a quiet place and sit or lay down. Most important is to make sure the position is comfortable. First, think of all your personal fears. The very secret thoughts of failure and then allow them to escape your body with every breath until your body is free from them.

Do not be surprised if you experience some overwhelming emotion the first time you try this part. You may cry or feel weak. The first time you do this, you may simply stop at this point once the fears and frustrations have left your body.

As you continue with your meditations for days, weeks, and years, you will not be as "penned up" with emotion and the pressure cooker that you might be right now will have been released and the effect will be less dramatic.

After releasing your fears, mentally embrace your strengths, picture or say the words that are associated with your personality. Picture or say your weaknesses and the words associated with them.

Then play out scenes or talk yourself through situations and challenges that you could face in daily life.

You might walk through the process of bringing up changes in the lodge. Picture the "Northern lights," the group of eternally grumpy past masters, sitting in the North part of the lodge and ever ready to bellow out the cry of change-kill, "That's not the way we've always done it."

Our first reaction might have been to convince ourselves that nothing is ever going to change or that a "few more Masonic funerals" are needed before any change might happen in the lodge.

With our new understanding of personalities and senses, let's put our secret psychology to work. We must recognize the personality types of the men in the North, instead of simply labeling them as bitter or old. The description might be accurate, but takes the easy road of not norming the situation typologically and applying our knowledge.

In our mental journey we determine that we have a couple of choices. We can sit back and analyze words they use and words we have heard them use, to norm them and ask the questions of ourselves. Or, we can approach them and ask the questions. For the sake of this example, we ask ourselves the questions about them and pay attention to their phraseology. We determine that two are When/Steadfast, one Why/ Dominant, and one What/Compliant.

For the sake of our discussion, we are trying to change one meeting a month to an education meeting where we do not read the minutes or pay bills, but simply have an enriching educational experience.

Remember, we are not going to sink to manipulation, but we are going to use our new knowledge of personalities to communicate in a way that is more effective.

We also determine that all the Brothers happen to be sight oriented.

Your *first* discussion with the lodge, that's right, it might take a some work, could go like this:

> "Worshipful Master, permission to address
> the lodge.

I have been watching things and looking around and notice that we don't have a lot of young Masons. I also saw that the ones we have had, have not come back. I decided that I would step up to the plate and provide a few ideas for helping with the issue and assisting in our lodge's future.

I have talked with some Brothers and found that a number of our younger members or potential members are looking for an educational experience. I don't like change for the sake of change and don't want to rush into things. But, if I could research some details I would like to approach the idea of having an educational night and seeing if this could help new members achieve success in the lodge and help the lodge achieve a future."

We are appealing to all four Brothers, using sight words, indicating we wish to meet a challenge but not to rush in and providing we do not want to change without first having some details and information.

Visualize the entire lodge meeting down to as much detail as you can, listen to yourself or picture yourself giving this address. Give yourself some obstacles, a Brother jumping up angry and doing a little name calling. Work through it calmly and effectively.

Give yourself a number of scenarios and different outcomes to work through.

As you take the technique from the mental world to the material one, you will have failures and frustrations.

There may be detractors and even enemies. Men of giant egos and little courage that will forever remain opposed to your success, to the success of their lodge, and in many ways their own spiritual success.

So what?

As we move forward, as we learn of ourselves, elevate our own spiritual self awareness, embrace our humanity and recognize and work on our own failures, we will achieve success.

Happiness and success are addicting in many ways. As we assist our Brothers by placing them in positions where they are naturally suited and communicate in ways that removes obstacles, you will succeed. Success will, in some ways, insulate you against detractors. Success is the best proof for successful ideas. As you achieve, those who gossip in the shadows will be silenced by those who have witnessed the successes you will share with your Brothers.

In the membership culture of beer and pizza Masonry, without the beer, it is difficult to fathom a Craft being accused of illuminism or the establishment of new world orders. Strangely enough, this is the next step in our to do list.

Establish a new world order through Masonry.

As the world still clashes under the symbols of religion and political differences, Masons gather around altars in lodge rooms around the world and pray with one another. That is power, true power.

The cross, the pentagram, the tau and serpent, the double tau, the hexagram, the sun, the moon, are all symbols used by various religions of the world. What else might they have in common? They are all symbols found in Masonry, they are all symbols that people have murdered for, and they are all symbols that billions of people have died for. Billions. The symbol is the most powerful language in the world and we guard the meaning to many of them within our simple lodge rooms and within the breast of our faithful members.

If you will permit me a bit of digression, I promise to return full circle and have a point in all of it.

I am going to expose the greatest secret in Masonry and its symbol. This particular secret has never been put into cipher and it is known only by those who are truly Princes of the Royal Secret.

Secrecy possesses extraordinary power. It produces courage. It is necessary for the existence of freewill. One of the simpler lessons of Masonry is that man is only as good as his word. Masonry makes it clear that he can control little in life except his own actions; but that if he can own himself, choose wisely, and keep his word, he will be an adept among men.

The man who achieves Mastery of the secret psychology will be so improved as to be able to accomplish great things in his life and, therefore, his community. All of this hinges on honesty with oneself and the application of speculative Masonry; therefore the secret psychology.
Know yourself, keep your word, and keep our Word.

Secrecy provides the balance and test of a man's freewill. He has the choice to simply practice silence or to discuss that which is improper, to gossip, to grumble. It is both a simple test and an extraordinary one. That is why Masonry is and should be a secret society. We guard a precious secret and our system of psychology.

The establishment of our new world order: A world void of intolerance, ignorance, and vile hatred.

Fundamentalism in all its forms has been the enemy of Masonry in all times. Regardless of the religion or government that it infects, fundamentalism is a virus all its own. It weaves itself into the minds of its adherents and convinces them that their particular view is the only view. Fundamentalism is the darkness by which the light of secret psychology shines.

Instead of the beauty of self awareness that results in tolerance; fundamentalism convinces the viral host that others are wrong, so much so, that they must die. Sitting in a Masonic lodge, among friends, among our Brothers, it is easy to convince ourselves that this is ridiculous, far off and that it would never and should never affect or infect us.

Nonetheless, grown men flying an airplane full of people into a building filled with even more people is utterly unthinkable. When you contemplate the fact that they saw this as a sacrifice to a loving God it becomes all the more frightening. It might be easy to slip back into our old ways and say, "This is an extreme example," or, "Thank God we are Christian." The wars in Bosnia and Herzegovina, terrorist actions in Ireland and Scotland, tribal wars among different Christian sects in Africa, and other recent and ongoing events provide evidence of the fact that Christian communities are just as willing to participate in such violence. No religion or political party is free of fundamentalism.

Our computers, cell phones, and iPods seem to conspire against us in lulling us in a false sense of security. We convince ourselves that in this modern time, in this fast paced and global economy, crime or the War on Drugs are our only enemies. It is easy to believe that the days of religious and political fundamentalist oppression are drawing to close. We easily convince ourselves, living in our democratic communities that freedom of speech, religion, and belief are all sacrosanct and that the only ones who don't believe such things are "living in the dark ages." There are 1.3 billion Muslims in the world making up over 20 percent of the world's population. It is estimated that 10 to 15 percent of the Muslim population or 100,300,000 to almost 200,000,000 members consider themselves fundamentalist. There are currently 2.1 billion Christians in the world. The fastest growing sect of Christianity in America, by far the most Christian nation, is fundamentalist Christianity.

In short, there are about half a billion people in the world that believe their religion should be the only religion and many of that same number believe it is God's will that the others they disagree with should perish.

Yet, in Masonic lodges around the world, men of all faiths, men who call themselves staunch Republicans, and stauncher Democrats, men who hunt all year long, and men who won't eat meat, gather, with smiles, around the altar of our Craft. They pray together, they break bread together, they drink together, they know one another's families, they care for each other when they are sick, and they mourn the loss of fellow Brothers together. They are Masons practicing Masonry.

Brethren please take a long look in the mirror. We are the new world order.

In a world where profane men still cannot progress beyond killing and going to war on behalf of their God, on behalf of the symbols mentioned at the start of this chapter; in a world where governments seek to destroy free speech; in a world where it is still taught in many churches that a loving God condemns everyone to hell who does not agree with some singular denomination or some particular pastor; in a world where people no longer know the names of their neighbors....you stand together in prayer and together in support of one another, unified under the same symbols that divide the rest of the world.

If we combine this beautiful tolerance with a new self knowledge, and labor in the world with it, we will change the world and we should.

A Mason, armed with the secret psychology of self, is an awesome force for bringing together the children of God. He is a strong working tool in building community, the forging of new bridges and paths to understanding, and the destroyer of obstacles to communication.

You have the secret, you have real power, and you have free will.

If we improve ourselves, we improve the universe.

A Lodge fitted Up for the Reception of the most Respectable MASTER.

Appendices

APPENDIX A - Humanum Genus

To the Patriarchs, Primates, Archbishops, and Bishops of the Catholic World in Grace and Communion with the Apostolic See,

The race of man, after its miserable fall from God, the Creator and the Giver of heavenly gifts, "through the envy of the devil," separated into two diverse and opposite parts, of which the one steadfastly contends for truth and virtue, the other of those things which are contrary to virtue and to truth. The one is the kingdom of God on earth, namely, the true Church of Jesus Christ; and those who desire from their heart to be united with it, so as to gain salvation, must of necessity serve God and His only-begotten Son with their whole mind and with an entire will. The other is the kingdom of Satan, in whose possession and control are all whosoever follow the fatal example of their leader and of our first parents, those who refuse to obey the divine and eternal law, and who have many aims of their own in contempt of God, and many aims also against God.

This twofold kingdom St. Augustine keenly discerned and described after the manner of two cities, contrary in their laws because striving for contrary objects; and with a subtle brevity he expressed the efficient cause of each in these words: "Two loves formed two cities: the love of self, reaching even to contempt of God, an earthly city; and the love of God, reaching to contempt of self, a heavenly one." At every period of time each has been in conflict with the other, with a variety and multiplicity of weapons and of warfare, although not always with equal ardor and assault. At this period, however, the partisans of evil seems to be combining together, and to be struggling with united vehemence, led on or assisted by that strongly organized and widespread association called the Freemasons. No longer making any secret of their purposes, they are now boldly rising up against God Himself. They are planning the destruction of holy Church publicly and openly, and this with the set purpose of utterly despoiling the nations of Christendom, if it were possible, of the blessings obtained for us through Jesus Christ our Saviour. Lamenting these evils, We are constrained by the charity which urges Our heart to cry out often to God: "For lo, Thy enemies have made a noise; and they that hate Thee have lifted up the head. They have taken a malicious counsel against Thy people, and they have consulted against Thy saints. They have said, 'come, and let us destroy them, so that they be not a nation.'

At so urgent a crisis, when so fierce and so pressing an onslaught is made upon the Christian name, it is Our office to point out the danger, to mark who are the adversaries, and to the best of Our power to make head against their plans and devices, that those may not perish whose salvation is committed to Us, and that the kingdom of Jesus Christ entrusted to Our charge may not stand and remain whole, but may be enlarged by an ever-increasing growth throughout the world.

The Roman Pontiffs Our predecessors, in their incessant watchfulness over the safety of the Christian people, were prompt in detecting the presence and the purpose of this capital enemy immediately it sprang into the light instead of hiding as a dark conspiracy; and , moreover, they took occasion with true foresight to give, as it were on their guard, and not allow themselves to be caught by the devices and snares laid out to deceive them.

The first warning of the danger was given by Clement XII in the year 1738, and his constitution was confirmed and renewed by Benedict XIV(4) Pius VII followed the same path; and Leo XII, by his apostolic constitution, Quo Graviora, put together the acts and decrees of former Pontiffs on this subject, and ratified and confirmed them forever. In the same sense spoke Pius VIII, Gregory XVI, and, many times over, Pius IX.

For as soon as the constitution and the spirit of the masonic sect were clearly discovered by manifest signs of its actions, by the investigation of its causes, by publication of its laws, and of its rites and commentaries, with the addition often of the personal testimony of those who were in the secret, this apostolic see denounced the sect of the Freemasons, and publicly declared its constitution, as contrary to law and right, to be pernicious no less to Christendom than to the State; and it forbade any one to enter the society, under the penalties which the Church is wont to inflict upon exceptionally guilty persons. The sectaries, indignant at this, thinking to elude or to weaken the force of these decrees, partly by contempt of them, and partly by calumny, accused the sovereign

Pontiffs who had passed them either of exceeding the bounds of moderation in their decrees or of decreeing what was not just. This was the manner in which they endeavored to elude the authority and the weight of the apostolic constitutions of Clement XII and Benedict XIV, as well as of Pius VII and Pius IX.(10) Yet, in the very society itself, there were to be found men who unwillingly acknowledged that the Roman Pontiffs had acted within their right, according to the Catholic doctrine and discipline. The Pontiffs received the same assent, and in strong terms, from many princes and heads of governments, who made it their business either to delate the masonic society to the apostolic see, or of their own accord by special enactments to brand it as pernicious, as, for example, in Holland, Austria, Switzerland, Spain, Bavaria, Savoy, and other parts of Italy.

But, what is of highest importance, the course of events has demonstrated the prudence of Our predecessors. For their provident and paternal solicitude had not always and every where the result desired; and this, either because of the simulation and cunning of some who were active agents in the mischief, or else of the thoughtless levity of the rest who ought, in their own interest, to have given to the matter their diligent attention. In consequence, the sect of Freemasons grew with a rapidity beyond conception in the course of a century and a half, until it came to be able, by means of fraud or of audacity, to gain such entrance into every rank of the State as to seem to be almost its ruling power. This swift and formidable advance has brought upon the Church, upon the power of princes, upon the public well-being, precisely that grievous harm which Our predecessors had long before foreseen. Such a condition has been reached that henceforth there will be grave reason to fear, not indeed for the Church - for her foundation is much too firm to be overturned by the effort of men - but for those States in which prevails the power, either of the sect of which we are speaking or of other sects not dissimilar which lend themselves to it as disciples and subordinates.

For these reasons We no sooner came to the helm of the Church than We clearly saw and felt it to be Our duty to use Our authority to the very utmost against so vast an evil. We have several times already, as occasion served, attacked certain chief points of teaching which showed in a special manner the perverse influence of Masonic opinions. Thus, in Our encyclical letter, Quod Apostolici Muneris, we endeavored to refute the monstrous doctrines of the socialists and communists; afterwards, in another beginning "Arcanum," We took pains to defend and explain the true and genuine idea of domestic life, of which marriage is the spring and origin; and again, in that which begins "Diuturnum,"(11) We described the ideal of political government conformed to the principles of Christian wisdom, which is marvelously in harmony, on the one hand, with the natural order of things, and, in the other, with the well-being of both sovereign princes and of nations. It is now Our intention, following the example of Our predecessors, directly to treat of the masonic society itself, of its whole teaching, of its aims, and of its manner of thinking and acting, in order to bring more and more into the light its power for evil, and to do what We can to arrest the contagion of this fatal plague.

There are several organized bodies which, though differing in name, in ceremonial, in form and origin, are nevertheless so bound together by community of purpose and by the similarity of their main opinions, as to make in fact one thing with the sect of the Freemasons, which is a kind of center whence they all go forth, and whither they all return. Now, these no longer show a desire to remain concealed; for they hold their meetings in the daylight and before the public eye, and publish their own newspaper organs; and yet, when thoroughly understood, they are found still to retain the nature and the habits of secret societies. There are many things like mysteries which it is the fixed rule to hide with extreme care, not only from strangers, but from very many members, also; such as their secret and final designs, the names of the chief leaders, and certain secret and inner meetings, as well as their decisions, and the ways and means of carrying them out. This is, no doubt, the object of the manifold difference among the members as to right, office, and privilege, of the received distinction of orders and grades, and of that severe discipline which is maintained.

Candidates are generally commanded to promise - nay, with a special oath, to swear - that they will never, to any person, at any time or in any way, make known the members, the passes, or the subjects discussed. Thus, with a fraudulent external appearance, and with a style of simulation which is always the same, the Freemasons, like the Manichees of old, strive, as far as possible, to conceal themselves, and to admit no witnesses but their own members. As a convenient manner of concealment, they assume the character of literary men and scholars associated for purposes of learning. They speak of their zeal for a more cultured refinement, and of their love for the poor; and they declare their one wish to be the amelioration of the condition of the masses, and to share with the largest possible number all the benefits of civil life. Were these purposes aimed at in real truth, they are by no means the whole of their object. Moreover, to be enrolled, it is necessary that the candidates promise and undertake to be thenceforward strictly obedient to their leaders and masters with the utmost submission and fidelity, and to be in readiness to do their bidding upon the slightest expression of their will; or, if disobedient, to submit to the direst penalties and death itself. As a fact, if any are judged to have betrayed the doings of the sect or to have resisted commands given, punishment is inflicted on them not infrequently, and with so much audacity and dexterity that the assassin very often escapes the detection and penalty of his crime.

But to simulate and wish to lie hid; to bind men like slaves in the very tightest bonds, and without giving any sufficient reason; to make use of men enslaved to the will of another for any arbitrary act ; to arm men's right hands for bloodshed after securing impunity for the crime - all this is an enormity from which nature recoils. Wherefore, reason and truth itself make it plain that the society of which we are speaking is in antagonism with justice and natural uprightness. And this becomes still plainer, inasmuch as other arguments, also, and those very manifest, prove that it is essentially opposed to natural virtue. For, no matter how great may be men's cleverness in concealing and their experience in lying, it is impossible to prevent the effects of any cause from showing, in some way, the intrinsic nature of the cause whence they come. "A good tree cannot produce bad fruit, nor a bad tree produce good fruit."(12) Now, the masonic sect produces fruits that are pernicious and of the bitterest savour. For, from what We have above most clearly shown, that which is their ultimate purpose forces itself into view - namely, the utter overthrow of that whole religious and political order of the world which the Christian teaching has produced, and the substitution of a new state of things in accordance with their ideas, of which the foundations and laws shall be drawn from mere naturalism.

What We have said, and are about to say, must be understood of the sect of the Freemasons taken generically, and in so far as it comprises the associations kindred to it and confederated with it, but not of the individual members of them. There may be persons amongst these, and not a few who, although not free from the guilt of having entangled themselves in such associations, yet are neither themselves partners in their criminal acts nor aware of the ultimate object which they are endeavoring to attain. In the same way, some of the affiliated societies, perhaps, by no means approve of the extreme conclusions which they would, if consistent, embrace as necessarily following from their common principles, did not their very foulness strike them with horror. Some of these, again, are led by circumstances of times and places either to aim at smaller things than the others usually attempt or than they themselves would wish to attempt. They are not, however, for this reason, to be reckoned as alien to the masonic federation; for the masonic federation is to be judged not so much by the things which it has done, or brought to completion, as by the sum of its pronounced opinions.

Now, the fundamental doctrine of the naturalists, which they sufficiently make known by their very name, is that human nature and human reason ought in all things to be mistress and guide. Laying this down, they care little for duties to God, or pervert them by erroneous and vague opinions. For they deny that anything has been taught by God; they allow no dogma of religion or truth which cannot be understood by the human intelligence, nor any teacher who ought to be believed by reason of his authority. And since it is the special and exclusive duty of the Catholic Church fully to set forth in words truths divinely received, to teach, besides other divine helps to salvation, the authority of its office, and to defend the same with perfect purity, it is against the Church that the rage and attack of the enemies are principally directed.

In those matters which regard religion let it be seen how the sect of the Freemasons acts, especially where it is more free to act without restraint, and then let any one judge whether in fact it does not wish to carry out the policy of the naturalists. By a long and persevering labor, they endeavor to bring about this result - namely, that the teaching office and authority of the Church may become of no account in the civil State; and for this same reason they declare to the people and contend that Church and State ought to be altogether disunited. By this means they reject from the laws and from the commonwealth the wholesome influence of the Catholic religion; and they consequently imagine that States ought to be constituted without any regard for the laws and precepts of the Church.

Nor do they think it enough to disregard the Church - the best of guides - unless they also injure it by their hostility. Indeed, with them it is lawful to attack with impunity the very foundations of the Catholic religion, in speech, in writing, and in teaching; and even the rights of the Church are not spared, and the offices with which it is divinely invested are not safe. The least possible liberty to manage affairs is left to the Church; and this is done by laws not apparently very hostile, but in reality framed and fitted to hinder freedom of action. Moreover, We see exceptional and onerous laws imposed upon the clergy, to the end that they may be continually diminished in number and in necessary means. We see also the remnants of the possessions of the Church fettered by the strictest conditions, and subjected to the power and arbitrary will of the administrators of the State, and the religious orders rooted up and scattered.

But against the apostolic see and the Roman Pontiff the contention of these enemies has been for a long time directed. The Pontiff was first, for specious reasons, thrust out from the bulwark of his liberty and of his right, the civil princedom; soon, he was unjustly driven into a condition which was unbearable because of the difficulties raised on all sides; and now the time has come when the partisans of the sects openly declare, what in secret among themselves they have for a long time plotted, that the sacred power of the Pontiffs must be abolished, and that the papacy itself, founded by divine right, must be utterly destroyed. If other proofs were wanting, this fact would be sufficiently disclosed by the testimony of men well informed, of whom some at other times, and others again recently, have declared it to be true of the Freemasons that they especially desire to assail the Church with irreconcilable hostility, and that they will never rest until they have destroyed whatever the supreme Pontiffs have established for the sake of religion.

If those who are admitted as members are not commanded to abjure by any form of words the Catholic doctrines, this omission, so far from being adverse to the designs of the Freemasons, is more useful for their purposes. First, in this way they easily deceive the simple-minded and the heedless, and can induce a far greater number to become members. Again, as all who offer themselves are received whatever may be their form of religion, they thereby teach the great error of this age-that a regard for religion should be held as an indifferent matter, and that all religions are alike. This manner of reasoning is calculated to bring about the ruin of all forms of religion, and especially of the Catholic religion, which, as it is the only one that is true, cannot, without great injustice, be regarded as merely equal to other religions.

But the naturalists go much further; for, having, in the highest things, entered upon a wholly erroneous course, they are carried headlong to extremes, either by reason of the weakness of human nature, or because God inflicts upon them the just punishment of their pride. Hence it happens that they no longer consider as certain and permanent those things which are fully understood by the natural light of reason, such as certainly are - the existence of God, the immaterial nature of the human soul, and its immortality. The sect of the Freemasons, by a similar course of error, is exposed to these same dangers; for, although in a general way they may profess the existence of God, they themselves are witnesses that they do not all maintain this truth with the full assent of the mind or with a firm conviction. Neither do they conceal that this question about God is the greatest source and cause of discords among them; in fact, it is certain that a considerable contention about this same subject has existed among them very lately. But, indeed, the sect allows great liberty to its votaries, so that to each side is given the right to defend its own opinion, either that there is a God, or that there is none; and those who obstinately contend that there is no God are as easily initiated as those who contend that God exists, though, like the pantheists, they have false notions concerning Him: all which is nothing else than taking away the reality, while retaining some absurd representation of the divine nature.

When this greatest fundamental truth has been overturned or weakened, it follows that those truths, also, which are known by the teaching of nature must begin to fall - namely, that all things were made by the free will of God the Creator; that the world is governed by Providence; that souls do not die; that to this life of men upon the earth there will succeed another and an everlasting life.

When these truths are done away with, which are as the principles of nature and important for knowledge and for practical use, it is easy to see what will become of both public and private morality. We say nothing of those more heavenly virtues, which no one can exercise or even acquire without a special gift and grace of God; of which necessarily no trace can be found in those who reject as unknown the redemption of mankind, the grace of God, the sacraments, and the happiness to be obtained in heaven. We speak now of the duties which have their origin in natural probity. That God is the Creator of the world and its provident Ruler; that the eternal law commands the natural order to be maintained, and forbids that it be disturbed; that the last end of men is a destiny far above human things and beyond this sojourning upon the earth: these are the sources and these the principles of all justice and morality. If these be taken away, as the naturalists and Freemasons desire, there will immediately be no knowledge as to what constitutes justice and injustice, or upon what principle morality is founded. And, in truth, the teaching of morality which alone finds favor with the sect of Freemasons, and in which they contend that youth should be instructed, is that which they call "civil," and "independent," and "free," namely, that which does not contain any religious belief. But, how insufficient such teaching is, how wanting in soundness, and how easily moved by every impulse of passion, is sufficiently proved by its sad fruits, which have already begun to appear. For, wherever, by removing Christian education, this teaching has begun more completely to rule, there goodness and integrity of morals have begun quickly to perish, monstrous and shameful opinions have grown up, and the audacity of evil deeds has risen to a high degree. All this is commonly complained of and deplored; and not a few of those who by no means wish to do so are compelled by abundant evidence to give not infrequently the same testimony.

Moreover, human nature was stained by original sin, and is therefore more disposed to vice than to virtue. For a virtuous life it is absolutely necessary to restrain the disorderly movements of the soul, and to make the passions obedient to reason. In this conflict human things must very often be despised, and the greatest labors and hardships must be undergone, in order that reason may always hold its sway. But the naturalists and Freemasons, having no faith in those things which we have learned by the revelation of God, deny that our first parents sinned, and consequently think that free will is not at all weakened and inclined to evil. On the contrary, exaggerating rather the power and the excellence of nature, and placing therein alone the principle and rule of justice, they cannot even imagine that there is any need at all of a constant struggle and a perfect steadfastness to overcome the violence and rule of our passions.

Wherefore we see that men are publicly tempted by the many allurements of pleasure; that there are journals and pamphlets with neither moderation nor shame; that stage-plays are remarkable for license; that designs for works of art are shamelessly sought in the laws of a so called verism; that the contrivances of a soft and delicate life are most carefully devised; and that all the blandishments of pleasure are diligently sought out by which virtue may be lulled to sleep. Wickedly, also, but at the same time quite consistently, do those act who do away with the expectation of the joys of heaven, and bring down all happiness to the level of mortality, and, as it were, sink it in the earth. Of what We have said the following fact, astonishing not so much in itself as in its open expression, may serve as a confirmation. For, since generally no one is accustomed to obey crafty and clever men so submissively as those whose soul is weakened and broken down by the domination of the passions, there have been in the sect of the Freemasons some who have plainly determined and proposed that, artfully and of set purpose, the multitude should be satiated with a boundless license of vice, as, when this had been done, it would easily come under their power and authority for any acts of daring.

What refers to domestic life in the teaching of the naturalists is almost all contained in the following declarations: that marriage belongs to the genus of commercial contracts, which can rightly be revoked by the will of those who made them, and that the civil rulers of the State have power over the matrimonial bond; that in the education of youth nothing is to be taught in the matter of religion as of certain and fixed opinion; and each one must be left at liberty to follow, when he comes of age, whatever he may prefer. To these things the Freemasons fully assent; and not only assent, but have long endeavored to make them into a law and institution.

For in many countries, and those nominally Catholic, it is enacted that no marriages shall be considered lawful except those contracted by the civil rite; in other places the law permits divorce; and in others every effort is used to make it lawful as soon as may be. Thus, the time is quickly coming when marriages will be turned into another kind of contract - that is into changeable and uncertain unions which fancy may join together, and which the same when changed may disunite.

With the greatest unanimity the sect of the Freemasons also endeavors to take to itself the education of youth. They think that they can easily mold to their opinions that soft and pliant age, and bend it whither they will; and that nothing can be more fitted than this to enable them to bring up the youth of the State after their own plan. Therefore, in the education and instruction of children they allow no share, either of teaching or of discipline, to the ministers of the Church; and in many places they have procured that the education of youth shall be exclusively in the hands of laymen, and that nothing which treats of the most important and most holy duties of men to God shall be introduced into the instructions on morals.

Then come their doctrines of politics, in which the naturalists lay down that all men have the same right, and are in every respect of equal and like condition; that each one is naturally free; that no one has the right to command another; that it is an act of violence to require men to obey any authority other than that which is obtained from themselves. According to this, therefore, all things belong to the free people; power is held by the command or permission of the people, so that, when the popular will changes, rulers may lawfully be deposed and the source of all rights and civil duties is either in the multitude or in the governing authority when this is constituted according to the latest doctrines. It is held also that the State should be without God; that in the various forms of religion there is no reason why one should have precedence of another; and that they are all to occupy the same place.

That these doctrines are equally acceptable to the Freemasons, and that they would wish to constitute States according to this example and model, is too well known to require proof. For some time past they have openly endeavoured to bring this about with all their strength and resources; and in this they prepare the way for not a few bolder men who are hurrying on even to worse things, in their endeavor to obtain equality and community of all goods by the destruction of every distinction of rank and property.

What, therefore, sect of the Freemasons is, and what course it pursues, appears sufficiently from the summary We have briefly given. Their chief dogmas are so greatly and manifestly at variance with reason that nothing can be more perverse. To wish to destroy the religion and the Church which God Himself has established, and whose perpetuity He insures by His protection, and to bring back after a lapse of eighteen centuries the manners and customs of the pagans, is signal folly and audacious impiety. Neither is it less horrible nor more tolerable that they should repudiate the benefits which Jesus Christ so mercifully obtained, not only for individuals, but also for the family and for civil society, benefits which, even according to the judgment and testimony of enemies of Christianity, are very great. In this insane and wicked endeavor we may almost see the implacable hatred and spirit of revenge with which Satan himself is inflamed against Jesus Christ. - So also the studious endeavor of the Freemasons to destroy the chief foundations of justice and honesty, and to co-operate with those who would wish, as if they were mere animals, to do what they please, tends only to the ignominious and disgraceful ruin of the human race.

The evil, too, is increased by the dangers which threaten both domestic and civil society. As We have elsewhere shown, in marriage, according to the belief of almost every nation, there is something sacred and religious; and the law of God has determined that marriages shall not be dissolved. If they are deprived of their sacred character, and made dissoluble, trouble and confusion in the family will be the result, the wife being deprived of her dignity and the children left without protection as to their interests and well being.-To have in public matters no care for religion, and in the arrangement and administration of civil affairs to have no more regard for God than if He did not exist, is a rashness unknown to the very pagans; for in their heart and soul the notion of a divinity and the need of public religion were so firmly fixed that they would have thought it easier to have city without foundation than a city without God. Human society, indeed for which by nature we are formed, has been constituted by God the Author of nature; and from Him, as from their principle and source, flow in all their strength and permanence the countless benefits with which society abounds. As we are each of us admonished by the very voice of nature to worship God in piety and holiness, as the Giver unto us of life and of all that is good therein, so also and for the same reason, nations and States are bound to worship Him; and therefore it is clear that those who would absolve society from all religious duty act not only unjustly but also with ignorance and folly.

As men are by the will of God born for civil union and society, and as the power to rule is so necessary a bond of society that, if it be taken away, society must at once be broken up, it follows that from Him who is the Author of society has come also the authority to rule; so that whosoever rules, he is the minister of God. Wherefore, as the end and nature of human society so requires, it is right to obey the just commands of lawful authority, as it is right to obey God who ruleth all things; and it is most untrue that the people have it in their power to cast aside their obedience whensoever they please.

In like manner, no one doubts that all men are equal one to another, so far as regards their common origin and nature, or the last end which each one has to attain, or the rights and duties which are thence derived. But, as the abilities of all are not equal, as one differs from another in the powers of mind or body, and as there are very many dissimilarities of manner, disposition, and character, it is most repugnant to reason to endeavor to confine all within the same measure, and to extend complete equality to the institutions of civic life. Just as a perfect condition of the body results from the conjunction and composition of its various members, which, though differing in form and purpose, make, by their union and the distribution of each one to its proper place, a combination beautiful to behold, firm in strength, and necessary for use; so, in the commonwealth, there is an almost infinite dissimilarity of men, as parts of the whole. If they are to be all equal, and each is to follow his own will, the State will appear most deformed; but if, with a distinction of degrees of dignity, of pursuits and employments, all aptly conspire for the common good, they will present the image of a State both well constituted and conformable to nature.

Now, from the disturbing errors which We have described the greatest dangers to States are to be feared. For, the fear of God and reverence for divine laws being taken away, the authority of rulers despised, sedition permitted and approved, and the popular passions urged on to lawlessness, with no restraint save that of punishment, a change and overthrow of all things will necessarily follow. Yea, this change and overthrow is deliberately planned and put forward by many associations of communists and socialists; and to their undertakings the sect of Freemasons is not hostile, but greatly favors their designs, and holds in common with them their chief opinions. And if these men do not at once and everywhere endeavor to carry out their extreme views, it is not to be attributed to their teaching and their will, but to the virtue of that divine religion which cannot be destroyed; and also because the sounder part of men, refusing to be enslaved to secret societies, vigorously resist their insane attempts.

Would that all men would judge of the tree by its fruit, and would acknowledge the seed and origin of the evils which press upon us, and of the dangers that are impending! We have to deal with a deceitful and crafty enemy, who, gratifying the ears of people and of princes, has ensnared them by smooth speeches and by adulation. Ingratiating themselves with rulers under a pretense of friendship, the Freemasons have endeavored to make them their allies and powerful helpers for the destruction of the Christian name; and that they might more strongly urge them on, they have, with determined calumny, accused the Church of invidiously contending with rulers in matters that affect their authority and sovereign power. Having, by these artifices, insured their own safety and audacity, they have begun to exercise great weight in the government of States; but nevertheless they are prepared to shake the foundations of empires, to harass the rulers of the State, to accuse, and to cast them out, as often as they appear to govern otherwise than they themselves could have wished. In like manner, they have by flattery deluded the people. Proclaiming with a loud voice liberty and public prosperity, and saying that it was owing to the Church and to sovereigns that the multitude were not drawn out of their unjust servitude and poverty, they have imposed upon the people, and, exciting them by a thirst for novelty, they have urged them to assail both the Church and the civil power. Nevertheless, the expectation of the benefits which was hoped for is greater than the reality; indeed, the common people, more oppressed than they were before, are deprived in their misery of that solace which, if things had been arranged in a Christian manner, they would have had with ease and in abundance. But, whoever strive against the order which Divine Providence has constituted pay usually the penalty of their pride, and meet with affliction and misery where they rashly hoped to find all things prosperous and in conformity with their desires.

The Church, if she directs men to render obedience chiefly and above all to God the sovereign Lord, is wrongly and falsely believed either to be envious of the civil power or to arrogate to herself something of the rights of sovereigns. On the contrary, she teaches that what is rightly due to the civil power must be rendered to it with a conviction and consciousness of duty. In teaching that from God Himself comes the right of ruling, she adds a great dignity to civil authority, and on small help toward obtaining the obedience and good will of the citizens. The friend of peace and sustainer of concord, she embraces all with maternal love, and, intent only upon giving help to mortal man, she teaches that to justice must be joined clemency, equity to authority, and moderation to lawgiving; that no one's right must be violated; that order and public tranquility are to be maintained; and that the poverty of those are in need is, as far as possible, to be relieved by public and private charity. "But for this reason," to use the words of St. Augustine, "men think, or would have it believed, that Christian teaching is not suited to the good of the State; for they wish the State to be founded not on solid virtue, but on the impunity of vice." Knowing these things, both princes and people would act with political wisdom, and according to the needs of general safety, if, instead of joining with Freemasons to destroy the Church, they joined with the Church in repelling their attacks.

Whatever the future may be, in this grave and widespread evil it is Our duty, venerable brethren, to endeavor to find a remedy. And because We know that Our best and firmest hope of a remedy is in the power of that divine religion which the Freemasons hate in proportion to their fear of it, We think it to be of chief importance to call that most saving power to Our aid against the common enemy. Therefore, whatsoever the Roman Pontiffs Our predecessors have decreed for the purpose of opposing the undertakings and endeavors of the masonic sect, and whatsoever they have enacted to enter or withdraw men from societies of this kind, We ratify and confirm it all by our apostolic authority: and trusting greatly to the good will of Christians, We pray and beseech each one, for the sake of his eternal salvation, to be most conscientiously careful not in the least to depart from what the apostolic see has commanded in this matter.

We pray and beseech you, venerable brethren, to join your efforts with Ours, and earnestly to strive for the extirpation of this foul plague, which is creeping through the veins of the body politic. You have to defend the glory of God and the salvation of your neighbor; and with the object of your strife before you, neither courage nor strength will be wanting. It will be for your prudence to judge by what means you can best overcome the difficulties and obstacles you meet with. But, as it befits the authority of Our office that We Ourselves should point out some suitable way of proceeding, We wish it to be your rule first of all to tear away the mask from Freemasonry, and to let it be seen as it really is; and by sermons and pastoral letters to instruct the people as to the artifices used by societies of this kind in seducing men and enticing them into their ranks, and as to the depravity of their opinions and the wickedness of their acts. As Our predecessors have many times repeated, let no man think that he may for any reason whatsoever join the masonic sect, if he values his Catholic name and his eternal salvation as he ought to value them. Let no one be deceived by a pretense of honesty. It may seem to some that Freemasons demand nothing that is openly contrary to religion and morality; but, as the whole principle and object of the sect lies in what is vicious and criminal, to join with these men or in any way to help them cannot be lawful.

Further, by assiduous teaching and exhortation, the multitude must be drawn to learn diligently the precepts of religion; for which purpose we earnestly advise that by opportune writings and sermons they be taught the elements of those sacred truths in which Christian philosophy is contained. The result of this will be that the minds of men will be made sound by instruction, and will be protected against many forms of error and inducements to wickedness, especially in the present unbounded freedom of writing and insatiable eagerness for learning.

Great, indeed, is the work; but in it the clergy will share your labors, if, through your care, they are fitted for it by learning and a well-turned life. This good and great work requires to be helped also by the industry of those amongst the laity in whom a love of religion and of country is joined to learning and goodness of life. By uniting the efforts of both clergy and laity, strive, venerable brethren, to make men thoroughly know and love the Church; for, the greater their knowledge and love of the Church, the more will they be turned away from clandestine societies.

Wherefore, not without cause do We use this occasion to state again what We have stated elsewhere, namely, that the Third Order of St. Francis, whose discipline We a little while ago prudently mitigated, should be studiously promoted and sustained; for the whole object of this Order, as constituted by its founder, is to invite men to an imitation of Jesus Christ, to a love of the Church, and to the observance of all Christian virtues; and therefore it ought to be of great influence in suppressing the contagion of wicked societies. Let, therefore, this holy sodality be strengthened by a daily increase. Amongst the many benefits to be expected from it will be the great benefit of drawing the minds of men to liberty, fraternity, and equality of right; not such as the Freemasons absurdly imagine, but such as Jesus Christ obtained for the human race and St. Francis aspired to: the liberty, We mean, of sons of God, through which we may be free from slavery to Satan or to our passions, both of them most wicked masters; the fraternity whose origin is in God, the common Creator and Father of all; the equality which, founded on justice and charity, does not take away all distinctions among men, but, out of the varieties of life, of duties, and of pursuits, forms that union and that harmony which naturally tend to the benefit and dignity of society.

In the third place, there is a matter wisely instituted by our fore fathers, but in course of time laid aside, which may now be used as a pattern and form of something similar. We mean the associations of guilds of workmen, for the protection, under the guidance of religion, both of their temporal interests and of their morality. If our ancestors, by long use and experience, felt the benefit of these guilds, our age perhaps will feel it the more by reason of the opportunity which they will give of crushing the power of the sects. Those who support themselves by the labour of their hands, besides being, by their very condition, most worthy above all others of charity and consolation, are also especially exposed to the allurements of men whose ways lie in fraud and deceit. Therefore, they ought to be helped with the greatest possible kindness, and to be invited to join associations that are good, lest they be drawn away to others that are evil. For this reason, We greatly wish, for the salvation of the people, that, under the auspices and patronage of the bishops, and at convenient times, these gilds may be generally restored. To Our great delight, sodalities of this kind and also associations of masters have in many places already been established, having, each class of them, for their object to help the honest workman, to protect and guard his children and family, and to promote in them piety, Christian knowledge, and a moral life. And in this matter We cannot omit mentioning that exemplary society, named after its founder, St. Vincent, which has deserved so well of the lower classes. Its acts and its aims are well known. Its whole object is to give relief to the poor and miserable. This it does with singular prudence and modesty; and the less it wishes to be seen, the better is it fitted for the exercise of Christian charity, and for the relief of suffering.

In the fourth place, in order more easily to attain what We wish, to your fidelity and watchfulness We commend in a special manner the young, as being the hope of human society. Devote the greatest part of your care to their instruction; and do not think that any precaution can be great enough in keeping them from masters and schools whence the pestilent breath of the sects is to be feared. Under your guidance, let parents, religious instructors, and priests having the cure of souls use every opportunity, in their Christian teaching, of warning their children and pupils of the infamous nature of these societies, so that they may learn in good time to beware of the various and fraudulent artifices by which their promoters are accustomed to ensnare people. And those who instruct the young in religious knowledge will act wisely if they induce all of them to resolve and to undertake never to bind themselves to any society without the knowledge of their parents, or the advice of their parish priest or director.

We well know, however, that our united labors will by no means suffice to pluck up these pernicious seeds from the Lord's field, unless the Heavenly Master of the vineyard shall mercifully help us in our endeavors. We must, therefore, with great and anxious care, implore of Him the help which the greatness of the danger and of the need requires. The sect of the Freemasons shows itself insolent and proud of its success, and seems as if it would put no bounds to its pertinacity. Its followers, joined together by a wicked compact and by secret counsels, give help one to another, and excite one another to an audacity for evil things. So vehement an attack demands an equal defense. Namely, that all good men should form the widest possible association of action and of prayer. We beseech them, therefore, with united hearts, to stand together and unmoved against the advancing force of the sects; and in mourning and supplication to stretch out their hands to God, praying that the Christian name may flourish and prosper, that the Church may enjoy its needed liberty, that those who have gone astray may return to a right mind, that error at length may give place to truth, and vice to virtue. Let us take our helper and intercessor the Virgin Mary, Mother of God, so that she, who from the moment of her conception overcame Satan may show her power over these evil sects, in which is revived the contumacious spirit of the demon, together with his unsubdued perfidy and deceit. Let us beseech Michael, the prince of the heavenly angels, who drove out the infernal foe; and Joseph, the spouse of the most holy Virgin, and heavenly patron of the Catholic Church; and the great Apostles, Peter and Paul, the fathers and victorious champions of the Christian faith. By their patronage, and by perseverance in united prayer, we hope that God will mercifully and opportunely succor the human race, which is encompassed by so many dangers.

As a pledge of heavenly gifts and of Our benevolence, We lovingly grant in the Lord, to you, venerable brethren, and to the clergy and all the people committed to your watchful care, Our apostolic benediction.

APPENDIX B - Sight, Sound, and Feeling Words
Sight Oriented Words

adhere	fade	light	rally
art	faint	lightening	red
beauty	fair	likeness	refined
black	fine	lime	represented
blaze	flare	limped	rich
blue	flashing	look	right
blurred	flaunting	lucid	scene
bright	flush	lucid	see
brilliant	fresh	luminous	setting
built	gather	lurid	shade
burst	ghostly	meet	shapeless
cast	glistening	messy	sharp
center	glowing	middle	shining
chaste	gray	neat	silver
clashing	green	neutral	sparkling
clear	halfway	nucleus	stain
cloudiness	heart	obscure	tidy
color	hub	opaque	tint
conceal	hue	orange	transparent
concealed	image	pale	trim
converge	imagine	pallid	unclear
crayon	indigo	painting	unclouded
dark	indistinct	pastel	uncolored
deep	inexact	perception	unfaded
delicate	ink	perspective	unsoiled

dingy	jet	picture	vague
distinct	key	pigment	view
dull	leaden	plain	vision
dye	left	point	violet
ebony	lemon	rainbow	vivid
			void
			varied
			variety
			wide
			white

Sound Oriented Words

accent	din	jeer	preach
acoustic	distinct	jest	quality
aloud	drum	jingle	quiet
amplify	drumming	joshing	racket
ask	dumb	jovial	radio
audible	ear	key	rattle
audience	echo	kidding	resonance
audio	explosion	laughter	resound
audition	faint	listen	ring
bang	frequency	loud	roar
bawl	full	maybe	roll
bellow	gagged	melody	rumble
blast	denial	messages	say
boom	gurgle	moduation	scream
broadcast	hark	muffled	screech
bubble	harmonize	muffler	shout

burble	harmony	music	shriek
cadence	hear	mute	shrill
call	hearer	name	silence
cheer	herald	news	sonic
chatter	hubbub	no	sound
communicate	hush	noise	speak
crash	inflection	noiseless	tone
crier	inform	oral	talk
cry	inquiry	ovation	thunderous
damper	interview	overhear	twang
deaf	intonation	patter	voice
deep	jabber	phonic	whoop
delight	jangle	pitch	yell
detonation	jargon	powerful	

Feeling Oriented Words

absorbing	earnest	heaving	profound
affected	electric	hot	polarizing
affection	emotion	ice	quick
agony	endurance	impetuous	quiver
alive	endure	important	rapt
anesthetic	enthusiasm	impressive	response
apart	experience	incisive	seething
ardent	excitable	indifference	sensation
arouse	excitement	inspiration	zeal
bear	tremor	keen	vitality
biting	fear	labor	sensuous
blush	feel	lethargy	shocking

boiling	fervent	like	silky
breathless	flaming	love	smart
brush	flat	lukewarm	soft
burning	flimsy	mellow	stir
callousness	flowing	mild	strong
chill	flush	move	suffer
close	flutter	touch	summary
trust	frigidity	warmth	sunny
coma	fumble	numb	supple
contact	glowing	numbness	sympathy
cordial	grasp	panting	taste
cruelty	grope	passion	tender
crumble	gushing	passionate	tepid
cutting	gusto	penetrating	tingling
deep	handle	pervading	throb
dull	hard	piercing	
eager	hasty	pleasure	
eagerness	trance	poignant	

This list was compiled by Dr. Steven Rhoads, of the International Training Academy of Linguistics and Kinesics. It is by no means exhaustive, but it does give the initial user an idea of how to norm people for typology, based on phraseology. Notice too, that some words overlap, as they have multiple perceptive approaches. "Faint", for instance, can describe a color or a feeling.

APPENDIX C

References for Further Research

"I feel like I can't find the answers I am looking for in Masonry and there are so many different things out there. Where can I look for quality Masonic information?"

As a Mason who is active in traveling and visiting other lodges, a true bibliophile of the worst kind and chronic e-Mason, I run into this question a lot. In hopes of providing some resources I have listed my personal favorites here to find out about several different topics to begin or continue your journey.

Masonry In General

Read the following books:

• *Morals and Dogma* by Albert Pike
• *Esoterika* by Albert Pike and prepared by Art De Hoyos
• *But I Digress* by Jim Tresner
• *Novo Clavis Esoterika* by Timothy Hogan or
  The Alchemical Keys to Masonic Ritual and *The 32 Secret Paths of Solomon* by the same author
• *The Meaning of Masonry* by W.L. Wilmshurst
• *The Secret Teachings of All Ages* by Manly P. Hall
• *The Way of the Craftsman* by Kirk MacNulty
• Albert Pike`s Lecture on Masonic Symbolism and A Second Lecture on Symbolism: *The Omkara and Other Ineffable Words*

Join the Scottish Rite Research Society even if you are not a Scottish Rite Mason at www.scottishrite.org

Visit and register at The Sanctum Sanctorum Masonic Educational Forum. This is a free website offering classes and guided discussions on alchemy, the nature of man from a quantum perspective, leadership, and a number of Masonic topics.
It is the only free regular Masons forum in the world where each member is personally vouched for via contact with their Grand Lodge and not just checked out via computer. Go to

www.thesanctumsanctorum.com and click the forums tab and then register. Be patient. As noted, each person must be personally vouched for.

Jungian Psychology

These recommendations are from a spiritual Jungian perspective:

Man and His Symbols by Carl Gustav Jung
Modern Man in Search of a Soul by Carl Gustav Jung
Psychology and Alchemy (Collected Works of C.G. Jung) by Carl Gustav Jung

Classes

Cliffporter@detectingdeception.com

Guided Self Study

Goto www.scottishrite.org and purchase the Master Craftsman program

Goto www.circesinternational.org and register for Circes. It is a 33 booklet self guided program through spiritual Jungian psychology. The program takes three years. Membership is well worth it and provides access to quarterly meetings in addition to the self guided study.

End Notes

[1] Haywood, H.L. 1923. *Symbolical Masonry.* New York, New York: George H. Doran.

[2] Pike, Albert 2003. *The Meaning of Masonry.* Layfayette, Louisiana: Cornerstone Book Publishers.

[3] Plautus. 1882. *The Comedies of Plautus.* Translated by Henry T. Riley. London: George Bell and Sons.

[4] Fellows, John. 1835. *An Exposition of the Mysteries or Religious Dogmas and Customs of Egyptians, Pythagoreans and Druids: With a inquiry into the origin and history of Freemasonry.* New York, New York: Gould, Banks and Co.

[5] Hall, Manly P. 1923. The Lost Keys of Freemasonry. New York, New York: Macoy Publishing and Masonic Supply Co.

[6] *Book of Jubalees. Chapter VI.* Translated by R.H. Charles from Ethiopian texts. Available from Sacred Texts: http://www.sacred-texts.com/bib/jub/jub00.htm

[7] Strong, James. 1979. *Strong's Exhaustive Concordance of the Bible with Greek and Hebrew Dictionaries.* Nashville, Tennessee: Royal Publishers and *Merriam-Webster's Collegiate Dictionary, Revision 11.* Springfield, Massachusetts: Merriam-Webster.

[8] *From Egypt to Babylon: The International Age 1550-500 BC.* 2008. Paul Collins Publisher. Cambridge, Massachusetts: Harvard University Press.

[9] Hogan, Timothy. 2007. *The Alchemical Keys To Masonic Ritual.* Raleigh, North Carolina: Lulu Press.

[10] Bombast, Aureolus Philippus Theophrastus. 1976. *The Hermetic and Alchemical Writings of Aureolus Philippus Theophrastus Bombast, of Hohenheim, called Paracelsus the Grea*t. Translated by A.E. Waite. Berkley, California: Shambhala.

[11] Pike, Albert. 1992. I*rano-Aryan Faith and Doctrine as Contained in the Zend-Avesta.* Facsimile of 1924 edition. Whitefish, Montana: Kessinger Publishing, LLC.

[12] Stavish, Mark. 1996. *The History of Alchemy in America.* Available from Hermetic.com http://hermetic.com/stavish/alchemy/history.html

[13] Pope Leo XIII. 1884. *Humanum Genus.* Vatican City: Libreria Editrice Vaticana. Availalbe from http://www.vatican.va/holy_father/leo_xiii/encyclicals/documents/hf_l-xiii_enc_18840420_humanum-genus_en.html

[14] Shamdasani, Shoos. 2004. *Jung and the Making of Modern Psychology: The Dream of a Science.* Cambridge, United Kingdom: Cambridge University Press.

[15] Jung, Carl G. 1995. *Memories, Dreams, Reflections.* New York, New York: Harper Collins.

[16] Rhoads, Dr. Steven. 2000. *Subconscious Communications curriculum for the International Training Academy of Linguistics and Kinesics.*

[17] Mackey, Albert G., M.D. 1914. *An Encyclopedia of Freemasonry and Its Kindred Sciences Comprising the Whole Range of Arts, Sciences, and Literature as Connected with the Institution.* New York, New York: The Masonic History Company.

[18] Gaiman, Neil. 2001. *Aermican Gods.* New York, New York: William Morrow and Co.

[19] Sickles, Daniel. 1868. *General Ahiman Rezon.* New York, New York: Masonic Publishing and Manufacturing Co. Available from Sacred Texts: http://www.sacred-texts.com/mas/gar/index.htm

[20] Rhoads, Dr. Steven. 2000. *Subconscious Communications curriculum for the International Training Academy of Linguistics and Kinesics.*

[21] Kubler-Ross, Elisabeth. 1996. *On Death and Dying.* London, England: Tavistock Publications.

[22] Kubler-Ross, Elisabeth and Kessler, David. 2007. *On Grief and Grieving: Finding the Meaning of Grief Through the Five Stages of Loss.* New York, New York: Scribner.

[23] Craig, Robert T. 1999. *Communication Theory as a Field.* Hoboken, New New Jersey: Blackwell Publishing.

[24] McNulty, W. Kirk. 2006. *Freemasonry: Symbols, Secrets, Significance.* London, UK: Thames & Hudson.

[25] Clark, David L., Bourtros, Nash N., and Mendez, Mario F. 2010. *Brain and Behavior: An Introduction to Behavioral Neuroanatomy.* Cambridge, United Kingdom: Cambridge University.

[26] Rhoads, Dr. Steven. 2000. Subconscious Communications curriculum for the International Training Academy of Linguistics and Kinesics.

[27] Onions, C.T., Friedrichen, G.W.S., and Burchfeld, R.W. 1966. *The Oxford Dictionary of English Etymology.* New York, New York: Oxford University Press.

[28] Shipley, Joseph. 2001. *The Origins of English Words: A Discursive Dictionary of Indo-European Roots.* Baltimore, Maryland: Johns Hopkins University Press.

[29] Oposopaus, John. 2001. *Guide to the Pythagorean Tarot.* Woodbury, Minnesota: Llewellyn Publications.

[30] Conan, Neal. 2005. *Why Not Fail?: Children, Grades and Self-Esteem.* NPR Radio Report. Available from http://www.npr.org/templates/story/story.php?storyId=4783882

[31] Morwood, James. 2008. *Oxford Latin Desk Dictionary*. New York, New York: Oxford University Press.

[32] Pike, Albert. 2005. Esoterika. Edited by Arturo de Hoyos. Scottish Rite Research Society: Washington, D.C.

[33] Hogan, Timothy. 2007. The Alchemical Keys To Masonic Ritual. Raleigh, North Carolina: Lulu Press.

[34] Ibid

[35] Ibid.